Counselling Adult Survivors of Childhood Abuse: From Hurting to Healing

Counselling Adult Survivors of Childhood Abuse: From Hurting to Healing

Edited by Zoë Pool and
Michael Jacobs

 Open University Press

Open University Press
McGraw-Hill Education
8th Floor, 338 Euston Road
London
England
NW1 3BH

email: enquiries@openup.co.uk
world wide web: www.openup.co.uk

and Two Penn Plaza, New York, NY 10121-2289, USA

First published 2017

Copyright © Zoe Pool and Michael Jacobs, 2017

All rights reserved. Except for the quotation of short passages for the purposes of criticism and review, no part of this publication may be reproduced, stored in a retrieval system, or transmitted, in any form or by any means, electronic, mechanical, photocopying, recording or otherwise, without the prior written permission of the publisher or a licence from the Copyright Licensing Agency Limited. Details of such licences (for reprographic reproduction) may be obtained from the Copyright Licensing Agency Ltd of Saffron House, 6–10 Kirby Street, London EC1N 8TS.

A catalogue record of this book is available from the British Library

ISBN-13: 978-0-335-26242-7
ISBN-10: 0-33- 526242-2
eISBN: 978-0-335-26243-4

Library of Congress Cataloging-in-Publication Data
CIP data applied for

Typeset by Transforma Pvt. Ltd., Chennai, India
Printed and bound by CPI Group (UK) Ltd, Croydon, CR0 4YY

Fictitious names of companies, products, people, characters and/or data that may be used herein (in case studies or in examples) are not intended to represent any real individual, company, product or event.

Praise for this book

'This is a seminal book. It is clearly and transparently written with a warm relational heart shining through the sensible and straightforward language. It is an intrinsic celebration of Moira Walker's legacy as well as a continuation of it. Professor Michael Jacobs and Zoe Pool and their talented hardworking contributors are to be deeply congratulated.'

Valerie Sinason, Founder of the Clinic for Dissociative studies, a child psychotherapist and adult psychoanalyst, poet and writer

'The stated hope of this book, to affirm and inspire the work of counsellors in the area of abuse, is absolutely fulfilled.

A thorough explanation of the needs of clients is outlined based on a clear summary of the impact of abuse. The therapeutic relationship and possibility of longer term therapy are found to be key factors in good outcomes.

Awareness of and ways of working with disassociation and taking into account attachment issues are not ignored and honest learning from practice is documented.

This book will be a useful resource to a range of people – counsellors, supervisors and managers can gain insight and inspiration from the learning shared especially in regard to setting up an agency, the impact of counselling in this area, the judicial and legal process and supervision.'

Tanya Orr, Chair of tag

'This book is an inspirational account of how voluntary counselling organisations can help survivors of Childhood Sexual Abuse (CSA) to recover and heal from trauma and abuse. It is a welcome and timely book given the increase in the number of disclosures from survivors of CSA, who need therapeutic support and yet have difficulty accessing service provision. This has created a desperate need for specialist counselling services that can address the specific needs of survivors of CSA and provide longer term therapeutic support.

This book will be invaluable to anyone working in such agencies to understand how they can help survivors to heal through one-to-one counselling and group work, and how to navigate and face the challenges of the criminal justice system. The chapters on the impact the work has on practitioners and the importance of supervision are essential reading for all those working in the field to minimize the risk of vicarious traumatisation. The book is a must for all those practitioners, voluntary counsellors, supervisors and support staff in voluntary agencies who provide much needed support to survivors of CSA.'

Christiane Sanderson, Senior Lecturer in Psychology, University of Roehampton, UK

Dedicated to the memory of Moira Walker (1948–2013) and the survivors of abuse who taught her and teach us

'I have worked as a therapist with abuse survivors for many years now and have also trained others to undertake this work, and supervised many working in this painful area. I am continually impressed by the tenacity and bravery not only of survivors but also of those who care for them, and work with them. A particular mention must go to those who put such enormous energy into setting up voluntary services that are literally life-savers for many, and they do it with few resources and often too little support. However, another feeling runs alongside. That is one of continuing horror at the scale of the problem; the forms it takes; the numbers involved; the appalling impact on the lives of so many adults as a result of childhood abuse, and the suffering and pain that is being inflicted, even as I write, on unimaginably large numbers of children.

'Although this horror may be seen to be reflected in society at large, it is yet to be translated into sufficient funding and sufficiently coherent and effective policies and service provision. If it is to have meaning it has to be backed up by money. And somehow we have to turn ourselves into a society that takes a wider responsibility for the well-being of children. They are our future and to ensure this they must be the responsibility of a larger community. Whilst services for the protection of children need to be scrutinized and need to be adequately resourced, the buck does not stop there. Children live in our streets, go to our schools, are our neighbours and part of our community. Turning a blind eye, seeing them as only the responsibility of designated others, is dangerous.'

Moira Walker
Abuse: Questions and Answers for Counsellors and Therapists (pp. xi–xii)

Contents

	List of editors and contributors	x
1	From hurting to healing: the agency perspective *Zoë Pool*	2
2	The development of a specialist agency *Kate Howe and Ann Daniel*	19
3	Survivors speak *Rosa Hubbard-Ford*	39
4	The practitioner's experience *Jane Zoega*	57
5	Working creatively with groups *Zoë Pool*	79
6	Survivors' experience of the judicial process *Zoë Pool and Ellie Maguire*	107
7	A practitioner's experience of the judicial process *Gail Longhurst*	129
8	Supervising practitioners working with abuse *Michael Jacobs*	142
	References	161
	Index	166

List of editors and contributors

Ellie Maguire has been involved with Dorset Action on Abuse for ten years as a fundraiser and administrator, and more recently as a trustee. She has five years' experience working with witnesses and victims of crime within a court setting, as the Service Delivery Manager of Citizens Advice Witness Service at Bournemouth Crown Court.

Ann Daniel, co-founder with Moira Walker of Dorset Action on Abuse, and a past Chair and Trustee, is a counselling supervisor, and jointly facilitates professional development meetings for voluntary counsellors at DAA. She has an MA in counselling and is a qualified, registered social worker and practice educator.

Kate Howe is a Senior Lecturer in Social Work at Bournemouth University and the current Chair of Trustees for Dorset Action on Abuse. She is immensely proud to have been involved with DAA for around eight years, as a supporter, trustee, and a co-facilitator of groups.

Rosa Hubbard-Ford is a psychotherapist with more than twenty-eight years' experience. She is a Trustee and trainer for Dorset Action on Abuse, and trains with other organizations in the UK and USA. Her specialist areas are working with survivors of childhood abuse, and helping those caught in the net of sex and pornography addictions.

Professor Michael Jacobs is a retired psychotherapist, and a patron of Dorset Action on Abuse. His late wife,

Moira Walker, was one of the co-founders of the organization. He supervises within DAA, as well as in private practice. He is the author and editor of a large number of counselling and psychotherapy texts.

Gail Longhurst, BSc, is a BACP-accredited counsellor and psychotherapist. She changed her career after more than two decades in the aviation industry. Previously, she focused on domestic abuse and honour crimes. Since joining Dorset Action on Abuse in 2008, her passion has become working with adult survivors of childhood abuse.

Zoë Pool is a UKCP-registered psychotherapist, with more than twenty years' experience working with survivors of childhood abuse and neglect. Since 2007 she has been the Service Director of Dorset Action on Abuse. Prior to becoming a psychotherapist, she was a performing arts teacher/facilitator and a community dance leader.

Jane Zoega is a qualified psychotherapist, registered with the BACP and the BPS with experience working in the private and voluntary sectors in the UK and abroad. She has an MSc in existential psychotherapy, and a BSc (Hons) in psychology. She works with individuals, couples and groups in private practice and for Dorset Action on Abuse.

This book is about one voluntary counselling organization, Hurting to Healing (formerly Dorset Action on Abuse), which specializes in helping adult survivors of all forms of childhood abuse – sexual, physical, emotional, and neglect. There is in one sense nothing special about Hurting to Healing, although it is a very special place for its clients and counsellors. However, it does work with a specialized issue, which has recently become very prominent in our society.

How Hurting to Healing functions, how it has developed from its small beginnings as Dorset Action on Abuse, what has been learned from and continues to be improved over time, the effects of its work on clients and counsellors, the range of its services, involvement with the police and the courts, and supervision – these different aspects represent what can only be a snapshot of a specific centre, which has something in common with other counselling organizations, but also aspects that are particular both to the people affected by abuse, and no doubt to its location and history.

It is the hope of the contributors – all members of this counselling community – that the chapters in this book both affirm the work of specialist counselling organizations like ours, and provide the inspiration for the work to develop in other parts of the country or in other counselling centres where those who have survived childhood abuse – and still carry the burden of it – can receive the help they so desperately need.

1

From hurting to healing: the agency perspective

Zoë Pool

> *Hurting to Healing as a secure base for therapeutic work • the evolving service • referral • initial meetings • boundaries • counselling • groups • working with dissociative phenomena • evaluation • developments*

A secure base

Hurting to Healing's mission is to help adult survivors overcome the difficulties they endure as a consequence of crimes committed against them as children. Some of our clients sought help elsewhere for their ongoing distress, but continued to suffer. Many experience great difficulty feeling safe in trusting others, especially in a strange environment: 'It is not easy for survivors to seek help: much of their childhood experience indicates that those whom society deems to be trustworthy are in reality not so' (Walker 2003: 69).

A frequent response when abuse is revealed is, in effect, to put the responsibility on the abused: 'Why didn't they tell someone?' Many survivors have tried to tell someone what was done to them, only to be disbelieved, and their experiences denied, belittled or ignored. Others have suffered silently for decades, telling no one. Some have been blamed because they did not disclose what was being done to them, others because they did.

Many survivors say they feel unable to function in their lives and relationships. Often plagued by flashbacks, they may be triggered unwillingly into re-experiencing traumatic memories. They feel cut off from the present, continually trapped and helpless in the past. Many harm themselves in different ways, in desperate but destructive attempts to cope. Many are now parents themselves and worry about the impact their difficulties may have upon their children. Many worry about how they can keep their children safe from potential abusers.

Hurting to Healing aims to offer safety within a comfortable therapeutic space at our centre, Seaforth House, which was established in 2009. Clients tell us that the pictures of nature on the walls of every room, the relaxing music playing in the waiting areas, the little dog that sometimes greets them, and the comfortably furnished counselling rooms, all contribute to an experience of being welcomed into a friendly, nurturing space where the difficult therapeutic work can begin (Figure 1.1). Nevertheless, we remain aware that the first steps from hurting towards healing are difficult for many survivors.

Figure 1.1 Counselling room at Seaforth House

Disclosure as a process

When clients attend Hurting to Healing for the first time, they have already made initial disclosures about childhood abuse and neglect. Nevertheless, they often are very anxious about taking the next steps towards accessing help, and feel threatened by the potential consequences of disclosure. They dread what might happen. Some fear that talking might resurrect memories from the past that will overwhelm them. Concerned about how they will react, they dread being unable to cope. Some clients disclose their worry that responsibilities, events or relationships in their life are already too difficult: focusing on what happened to them as a child may make things unmanageable. Many say they feel they are bad – they experience chronic shame, and fear judgement or blame by others, including the counsellor.

Sometimes, memories are only partial, and the client fears what else she or he may remember, or what might emerge. Their memories may be so sketchy that they wonder if 'it' actually happened. Some feel reluctant to disclose little more than the fact that something was done to them; others may have an overwhelming need to pour out in great detail their experiences of being abused and neglected.

Referral

The majority of clients are referred or signposted to Hurting to Healing by NHS practitioners – including community mental health teams (CMHTs), general practitioners (GPs), psychiatrists, IAPT (Increasing Access to Psychological Therapies) practitioners, psycho-sexual therapists, and pain clinics – who recognize Hurting to Healing as a specialist agency for adult survivors. Other referrals come from the police, Social Services, the Probation Service, Victim Support, Rape Crisis, drug and alcohol agencies, family centres, health visitors, the Samaritans, private counsellors, and self-referrals. Many clients referred by the NHS have psychiatric diagnoses that include borderline or emotionally unstable personality disorder, bi-polar mood disorder, complex post-traumatic stress disorder (PTSD), schizophrenia, and dissociative disorders.

Links with the Samaritans means clients in crisis, or at risk of suicide, can be offered a Samaritan 'buddy' to support them between sessions. The Victim Support/Witness Service also provides additional support for clients while they are Crown Prosecution Service (CPS) prosecution witnesses.

Clients referred from within the NHS often say they were offered only short-term interventions such as cognitive behavioural therapy (CBT). Some report being denied any therapy at all and having been discharged by their doctors, even when they continue to express suicidal ideation. Even when longer-term approaches have been provided within the NHS, such as dialectical behaviour therapy or longer-term cognitive analytical therapy, clients report that their need to address what happened to them in the past has been actively discouraged by the therapist. One client, Lesley, said:

> *I was on an NHS waiting list for eighteen months; I'd told them about being abused, but when it came to it, they only offered me six sessions. When the therapy began, she told me I could only focus on the present. She wouldn't let me talk about the past. What use is six sessions or even six months? They gave me anti-depressants, anti-psychotics, and diazepam for emergencies, but none of them helped me to actually cope.*

From the point of referral, we clarify what clients can expect from Hurting to Healing and from their counsellor, including Hurting to Healing's commitment to uphold:

- Robust, ethical principles and safe practice
- Anti-discriminatory and anti-oppressive practice – with equality and respect for individual differences
- Confidentiality, and clarification of its limits
- Boundaries of counselling – length of contract and of sessions, clarity about payment for sessions, reviews, breaks, and endings
- Clarity about policies regarding requests for reports or letters of support to be sent to other professionals.

The initial meeting

A primary aim of our first meetings with clients is to facilitate manageable levels of initial disclosure. We take care not to encourage the client to disclose too much during this meeting. As childhood memories may be disclosed, the aim is to contain the client safely within the process and minimize the likelihood of becoming overwhelmed. 'Whenever we work with an adult who has been abused as a child, we also work with the frightened and hurt child they once were, and who is still hiding within' (Walker 1992: 165).

We focus on welcoming the whole person and their experience, rather than identifying diagnostic criteria. Many clients tell us that a mental health label is disempowering and unhelpful to them, especially when no meaningful therapy has been provided. We acknowledge throughout the first meeting that we understand that this may be a difficult and potentially intrusive experience. We explain that the aim of gathering information and the initial meeting is to get a better understanding of what a client's needs are, and how we might be able to help.

Prior to the first meeting, we ask clients to complete a form, which asks for background information, and a dissociative experiences questionnaire. In the face-to-face meeting with an experienced therapist at our centre, we ask clients about their current and past life experiences, personal and family relationships past and present, whether they have children under the age of 16, and whether they are in paid work or do voluntary work. We ask for a brief description of abuses or neglect in childhood, and how they coped while growing up, including their efforts to protect themselves, as well as how they cope now. We wonder if they have previously disclosed their abuse, and what response they had if they did. We check out emotional experiences in the past and present, mental and physical health, current medication, and signs or awareness of dissociative states and phenomena. We probe previous therapeutic interventions and, if there has been an NHS diagnosis, how they felt about that. We also ask about their social lives and participation in the community, their self-confidence and self-esteem. And a very important question concerns their hopes for the future. We assess their suitability, readiness, and ability to participate in what we can offer. We consider signs of post-traumatic stress reactions, self-harm, phobias, flashbacks, nightmares, mood swings, physical sensations, and problems with alcohol, substances, eating or other numbing behaviours.

We consider carefully the extent to which the client is ready and able to make the commitment to attend counselling once a week for up to a year. In assessing whether it is the right time for the client to undertake counselling or therapeutic group work, we weigh up whether they are stable *enough*, whether any other presenting problem needs to be addressed first, such as substance or alcohol abuse, other addictions, and physical health. We check whether there is anything else that might disrupt their commitment, such as childcare, work or a course of study, and what support they have. Finally, we seek to determine what their hopes are from counselling, and whether these are realistic, together with signs they can develop a trusting relationship with a counsellor. We consider just as carefully which counsellor might be best suited to working with a particular client.

The client is placed on a waiting list and, when a suitable counselling space is available, we offer an introductory period of between four and six weeks. Clients are expected to pay an agreed amount for every session, including missed sessions, *according to their means*. Counsellors later review the payment with clients, which can be increased or decreased if clients' circumstances change. Although it is Hurting to Healing's belief that therapy should be free for those who have survived any form of childhood abuse, a condition of Lottery funding is that clients are asked to contribute towards the cost of their counselling and therapy. Some clients understandably feel penalized by this: on top of the symptoms and distress that are the consequences of abuse, they are now expected to pay for therapy to recover. One client, Jim, said:

> *It's not right. It's not fair. I went to my GP because I couldn't get over it. I'd tried, but I couldn't get my*

past out of my head. The NHS is supposed to help their patients but they don't. They sent me down to you but I've got to pay. I feel like I'm paying to mend something I had no control over.

But it is our reality, and we have to comply.

The introductory period of counselling

A four- to six-week introductory period of counselling was introduced when it became clear some clients struggled to make the commitment to attend every week. During this time, we ask the counsellor to consider with their client how they are beginning to relate to each other, and whether the client is beginning to settle into the counselling process and relationship. It is important the client understands the commitment to weekly sessions, their financial commitment, and whether their expectations are realistic. The counsellor considers any experience of, or signs of, dissociation in the sessions, such as flashbacks, regression to child or fragile self-states, blanking out or long silences. The counsellor is also asked to consider whether the client can manage any emotional distress *sufficiently* between sessions, whether once-weekly sessions are adequate or whether the client needs additional support from the CMHT crisis team. We also ask whether the counsellor feels able to continue working with the client.

In addition to those considered in the initial meeting, reasons for poor attendance or engagement in the process include changes in medication, an overwhelming increase in distress, such as through flashbacks or self-harm, fears about changes in relationships, fear of what may emerge in counselling, and difficulties trusting the counsellor.

During this initial period, the counsellor and client can agree to continue, with a further review at twelve weeks or sooner. If difficulties with attendance or financial contribution are an issue, ways forward are considered. In some cases a referral to the GP, CMHT or a psychiatrist may be made. Ideally, any course of action is mutual. If, for any reason, the client cannot work with the assigned counsellor but wants to continue with Hurting to Healing, the client is referred back to the service director, who offers the chance to discuss alternative options. If the work is to end at this point, the counsellor completes an ending review with the client. However, the door is left open for the client to return at a later date.

The counselling team

Volunteer counsellors are recruited through our website, local colleges, professional counselling organizations, volunteer bureaux, and by word of mouth. Applications are encouraged from volunteers from diverse backgrounds, languages, and cultures. From 2008 to 2016, seventy-five volunteer counsellors offered a two-year commitment of three counselling sessions per week plus fortnightly supervision.

Counsellors have to have the skills and knowledge to work with survivors. We recruit only counsellors who hold a nationally recognized qualification (i.e. counselling diploma or degree), or who are in the final stages of qualifying. Registration with a professional organization such as the British Association for Counselling and Psychotherapy (BACP) is essential, as are a current Disclosure and Barring Service (DBS) check, personal indemnity insurance, and two good references. Several counsellors who are themselves survivors of childhood abuse have successfully overcome their difficulties and trained in counselling, since they feel motivated to help other survivors.

Counsellors undertake an induction and complete our own training course in abuse and trauma counselling skills, which includes the theory and practice of working therapeutically with clients' dissociating self-states and fragile processes. There is a counsellor handbook, which is regularly updated and includes all Hurting to Healing policies. Student counsellors on placement complete agreement forms, which are also signed by their tutor. Following client sessions, all counsellors participate in a 'debrief' of their work in groups of three. In addition, in accordance with BACP requirements, experienced supervisors provide fortnightly ninety-minute sessions of supervision in pairs or groups of three. Supervisors also have regular meetings, which are facilitated by an experienced supervisor. We regularly hold continuing professional development (CPD) seminars for volunteers to develop their expertise in working with survivors.

Given the intensity of this work, care is taken to ensure that our counsellors are always adequately supported. We recognize the potential for vicarious trauma, and endeavour to minimize this where possible. All counsellors have contact details of Hurting to Healing supervisors in case of emergency. They are encouraged to prioritize their own self-care and, if not currently in therapy, to seek personal support if or when necessary. Chapter 4 considers the experiences of our practitioners.

Counselling perpetrators is a particular skill. It is a myth that adults who were abused as children inevitably become abusers. Most Hurting to Healing clients are not abusers. Hurting to Healing is unequivocal that all forms of childhood abuse are wrong, and has clear policies regarding child protection that all clients are made aware of at assessment. In recent years, however, there have been more referrals from survivors of childhood abuse who have abused children and been convicted for their offences. They recognize the roots of their offending behaviour and want help for the abused child within them. 'It helps to remember that an abuser who has been victimized has also been hurt and damaged, and has not yet resolved their own abuse' (Walker 2003: 102). Not all counsellors are willing to work with perpetrators, but we endeavour to raise awareness in our volunteers and others about the complexities and ethical dilemmas involved in working with this client group.

Therapeutic practice

Although there are numerous models for working with traumatized survivors of childhood abuse, there is no evidence that one single therapeutic approach is better than another. There is, however, consensus that establishing safety, maintaining ethical, stabilizing boundaries, and developing empathic attunement in a therapeutic relationship are essential. We have practitioners trained in several different theoretical approaches: psychodynamic, person-centred, existential, integrative, and transpersonal. Our counsellors may be a part of group supervision with a supervisor and peers who work with a different theoretical approach.

Central to the work in all these models is the essential, shared factor of a containing, therapeutic relationship over a minimum of one year. As an attachment psychotherapist, Sue Richardson writes: 'Therapy needs to provide the means of transforming ineffective or non-existent internal caregiving into an internal supportive environment' (2002: 155). The initial aim for the work is always to facilitate possibilities for safety and trust within the relationship and process, offering clients as much control and autonomy as is possible in the context. 'The client needs assurance that they can proceed at a pace that is comfortable, and that there will be no pressure to disclose anything that cannot yet be tolerated' (Walker 1992: 147). It takes time for clients to feel stable and safe enough in the therapeutic relationship and process to begin the work of addressing their past. Counsellors also abstain from seeking premature change or immediate cessation of problematic, destructive behaviours. Nonetheless, as Bromberg writes, trauma survivors 'are optimally released from the crippling effects of their traumatic past when they are simultaneously released from the grip of their own self-cure (i.e. what they continue to do to themselves and to others in order to cope with a past that continues to haunt them)' (2014: 648).

Working with dissociative phenomena

Working with abuse requires particular knowledge and skill, particularly in the area of dissociative phenomena. Hurting to Healing knows from its clients that there is a link, as many studies have shown, between adverse childhood experiences and dissociative states. As Moira Walker, who conducted interviews with survivors who had developed multiple personalities, reflected: 'the abuse they had experienced was so severe that developing multiple personalities seemed an unconscious life-saving strategy. I was left with the question of whether they would have survived without it' (Walker 1992: 114). Dissociative states are essential for survival, and are manifest in Hurting to Healing's clients across a continuum from moderate to extreme (MIND 2013). With this in mind, counsellors are trained to pay close attention to their clients' awareness and experience of dissociative phenomena and how these adversely affect their clients' day-to-day lives (see also Herman 1997; Sinason 2002, 2012a, 2012b; Walker 2003; Dell and O'Neill 2014).

Until recently, formal diagnoses of dissociative 'disorders' in Dorset were rare. Many of our clients tell us that their struggles with dissociative self-states have been ignored, misunderstood, denied, and misdiagnosed. Over the years, numerous clients who have struggled with extreme dissociative distress have been referred to Hurting to Healing by psychiatrists who have denied any possibility of dissociative identities or dissociative disorders. A number of clients, who presented at Hurting to Healing experiencing severe dissociative difficulties, reported that they had been diagnosed with personality disorders and prescribed antipsychotic medication, which did nothing to help the voices they heard. Some but not all of Hurting to Healing's clients find diagnoses, labels, and structures helpful. When their dissociating alter egos or states are finally validated, as they are within Hurting to Healing services, clients become more able to stabilize and undertake long-term therapy.

A number of clients referred to us have in addition experienced ritual abuse by cults or paedophile rings. These clients need a very experienced therapist to work with them; they also need the security of longer-term work, in some cases for at least five years, which Hurting to Healing tries to provide.

Hurting to Healing facilitated groups

Group work has been a key part of Hurting to Healing's services from the beginning. Safety is always our primary concern, though there have been mistakes along the way in trying out self-help groups without some form of oversight or facilitation. Ways of facilitating groups have developed from learning what does and what does not help. Client feedback on their needs and concerns is very important. Facilitators need to have an understanding of the consequences of abuse and are either qualified counsellors with group work experience or experienced group facilitators. We run training in group work and provide regular support and supervision for facilitators.

Nevertheless, many clients say after one-to-one counselling that they need additional support to overcome their social isolation, feelings of stigma, and discomfort being with others. They express their need to build more confidence and resilience in order to become more actively engaged in relationships and the community. In addition to our creative therapies programme (see Chapter 5), we offer support through different types of time-limited, facilitated therapeutic groups that address specific topics reflecting clients' difficulties and needs. The agreed focus for each group aims to enhance motivation and to encourage a greater connectedness with others. Survivors of childhood abuse often find groups particularly challenging initially, since fears of being judged, shamed, bullied, attacked, or rejected by others can be triggered. They struggle to trust that it can be safe to show vulnerability, or to express oneself assertively. *Being with Others*, a six-week therapeutic group, addresses the challenges and underlying fears of being seen and heard by others.

Several clients have said that, following their time with Hurting to Healing, they have felt motivated to become more physically active and adventurous, to lose weight, to increase their fitness, or to discontinue anti-depressant medication. We are currently piloting outdoor, nature-based therapeutic groups that encourage physical activity with others in the natural environment, encouraged by current national initiatives that emphasize the beneficial role that the arts, physical activity, and the natural environment play in improving mental health, confidence, self-esteem, social interaction, and wellbeing (RSPH Working Group 2013).

Review and evaluation

Our aim as a specialist agency is that our clients will experience improved psychological wellbeing, be better able to cope with challenges, and finally to enjoy their lives. We review their experience of Hurting to Healing services with reference to outcomes. The review processes are beneficial therapeutically, and also essential for reporting on our work to our funders, who require statistics that demonstrate how we are helping our clients. We compare the numbers of our clients with our estimates, and report regularly to funders and to Hurting to Healing trustees.

Monitoring informs our forward planning, including for new/additional therapeutic groups, and recruitment of additional counsellors.

Clients' opinions of how Hurting to Healing has helped them are described in Chapter 3. At reviews during and at the end of counselling, clients are asked whether the problems they asked for help with have improved, and if so to what extent, or if any have remained the same or become worse. Aspects that need ongoing attention are addressed in terms of future help. The final review includes open questions that allow clients to describe whether and how Hurting to Healing services are of benefit (with responses recorded to identify common themes or suggestions), and more focused questions that enable statistics to be produced, important of course for funding.

From the statistical data from ending reviews received between October 2014 and August 2015, clients at assessment spoke of the following difficulties or symptoms (in many cases more than one): mood swings (94%), anxiety/fear (84%), depression (82%), difficulty sleeping (77%), flashbacks (76%), panic attacks (62%), phobias (50%), eating disorders (46%), self-harm (29%), alcohol misuse (27%), and substance misuse (16%). And the following personal or social difficulties were present at assessment and rated as 'poor' or 'not so good': self-esteem (85%), confidence (81%), isolation/loneliness (78%), social withdrawal (75%), absence of social life (72%), family relationships (65%), quality of life (64%), partner relationships (50%), friendships (38%), and staying in work (33%).

By the end of counselling, 79% of clients had experienced an improvement in at least half of their difficulties/symptoms as listed above, and most clients had experienced improvements in their personal/social difficulties: improvement in partner relationships (94%), ability to maintain work (91%), family relationships (90%), social life (89%), confidence (80%), quality of life (78%), self-esteem (74%), not withdrawing socially (77%), feeling less isolated and lonely (75%). At the end of counselling, 90% of clients were 'happy' or 'very happy' with the service they received (81% were 'very happy') and 93% would recommend Hurting to Healing.

As a result of Hurting to Healing's therapeutic services, adult survivors say that they are able to access long-term specialist help that is unavailable on the NHS, experience a reduction in numerous emotional difficulties/symptoms, feel more confident and have improved self-esteem, feel able to be more active in the community, experience an improvement in relationships with family, friends and partners, are more able to seek voluntary or paid work, are more able to express their feelings, make decisions and cope with challenges, no longer feel a sense of being alone in their experiences, are able to accept that the abuse was not their fault, and have a better understanding of themselves and the impact of abuse.

Developments and outreach

As we learn from our experience, so our services develop and evolve. We continue to expand our presence in the wider community, to respond to survivors' needs where we can, and to raise awareness of the impact of childhood abuse and trauma and the need for suitable services. Each year we provide a placement to Bournemouth University social work students, allowing them to develop important knowledge and skills in their chosen profession. Hurting to Healing clients, as 'experts by experience', help to facilitate training sessions for them. Hurting to Healing is an affiliate member of First Person Plural, a charity led by volunteers with lived experience of childhood-trauma-related, complex dissociative conditions.

Following an extensive evaluation in 2014–15 of all Hurting to Healing services, many clients welcomed the possibility of staying in contact with Hurting to Healing after their therapeutic care came to an end. We have now recruited a client liaison volunteer whose role is to facilitate and encourage beneficial relationships between current and former service users and Hurting to Healing, to coordinate the development of a group of Hurting to Healing 'experts by experience', to gather feedback from former clients regarding their experience of Hurting to Healing services, and to be a conduit for suggestions for possible changes or improvements.

> **Conclusion**
>
> Hurting to Healing endeavours to be a supportive community, and volunteers are encouraged to participate in all Hurting to Healing's activities when they can, including training, fundraising, outreach, and social events. We value reciprocal agreements, both informal and formal, with relevant organizations that help to achieve our outcomes. Collaboration strengthens better understanding of childhood-trauma-related, dissociative conditions among professionals and others in the statutory, voluntary, and private sectors, with the aims of improving therapeutic services and public awareness, and positive outcomes for those who are affected. This, too, is the aim of this book and the chapters that follow.

2

The development of a specialist agency

Kate Howe and Ann Daniel

> *The prevalence of childhood abuse • its effects on adults • the need for specialist services • first steps to starting an agency • creating a counselling service • the first year and the first difficulties • funding • the next stage • training and conferences • evolution of Dorset Action on Abuse into Hurting to Healing*

Introduction

Dorset Action on Abuse (DAA) owes its existence to the insight, passion, and drive of a group mainly of women, led by Dr Moira Walker, who were increasingly concerned that survivors of childhood abuse suffer mental ill-health, social exclusion, and disadvantage as a direct result of their childhood experiences. This concern was increased by the recognition that the generic health and social care services did not meet their needs, and specialist services offering skilled support did not exist.

In 2003, Moira was appointed Reader in the Institute of Health and Community Studies at Bournemouth University. She was a Fellow of the British Association for Counselling and Psychotherapy (BACP) and had worked with survivors of abuse for many years as a practitioner, trainer, and supervisor. She had also written widely on the subject and on the basis of that work obtained her doctorate at a later date. Prior to her appointment at Bournemouth University, Moira had been working in Dorset as a specialist therapist with vulnerable children. She felt passionately about the lack of services for adult survivors of abuse, and was the catalyst and driving force behind the creation of Dorset Action on Abuse.

The need for such a service in Dorset was and is obvious, just as it is in all parts of the country. Although the scale of child abuse is now better acknowledged, current statistics show that childhood abuse is increasing. In 2010, there were 46,709 children on the child protection register or subject to child protection plans (Radford et al. 2011); by 2014, this had risen to 56,231. However, it is difficult to quantify the exact scale of childhood abuse, and many believe that most statistics are a substantial underestimate. In 2010, for example, 2,465 children were the subject of a child protection plan under the category of sexual abuse, against 17,727 sexual offences against children aged under 16 recorded by the police (Bunting 2014). We know that child protection statistics record only those children who have been in contact with social services, and it is clear from DAA's work with adult survivors that a large number are not included.

The British Crime Survey gives yet another picture. In 2010–11, it estimates that there were 576,000 violent incidents against children between the ages of 10 and 15, but states that only a minority were reported to the police. Additionally, Bunting (2014) makes a quite horrifying claim, based on her research, when she estimates that only 19% of sexual offences and 24% of physically violent offences are detected.

Furthermore, there is evidence from a number of research studies that disclosure of sexual abuse in particular is often delayed, sometimes until many years later, when the survivor is an adult. For example, a study in 2000 found that, of 2,689 young people known to the NSPCC, 72% were sexually abused as children and did not tell anyone at the time, and 31% of them had still not disclosed to anyone by early adulthood (Cawson et al. 2000).

A review of research by Gilbert et al. (2008) on the prevalence of child maltreatment for the medical journal *The Lancet* found that the substantiated child maltreatment cases referred each year to child protection services concerned 1% of children in the population, yet research indicates that between 4 and 16% of children experience physical abuse each year, 10% experience psychological abuse, between 1 and 15% are neglected, and between 10 and 25% are exposed to domestic violence directed at a parent (Gilbert et al. 2008).

It is clear from this short exploration into the statistics that child abuse is a hidden crime with victims whose suffering is invisible – and there is the even less recognized fact that the effects last long into adulthood, requiring more services than have been or are currently available.

Effects of childhood abuse in adulthood

Direct consequences of childhood abuse in adulthood have been documented by a number of clinicians and researchers, including Moira Walker (2003) and Christiane Sanderson (2006). These include self-harm, panic attacks, sexual difficulties, post-traumatic stress, depression, suicide, substance abuse, eating disorders, inability to maintain work, homelessness, prostitution, criminality, difficulties parenting, and the continuing cycle of domestic violence. Clear links have been found between the experience of childhood abuse and these emotional and social problems.

Studies have also shown that there is a high proportion of survivors in the psychiatric population: Ainscough and Toon (2000), for example, state that 50% of women and 23% of men receiving psychiatric help have been sexually abused. A study by Spataro and colleagues demonstrated a clear link between child sexual abuse and serious mental health disturbances in both childhood and adult life:

> *In our view, however, child sexual abuse often emerges from a nexus of adversity and its impact is mediated by a range of family, social, psychological and biological variables. The doubts about whether there are true associations between child sexual abuse and significant disturbances of mental health both in childhood and in adult life, which continue to be raised ... can now be answered unequivocally in the affirmative.*
> (Spataro et al. 2004: 420)

As research continues, these effects are being better understood. For example, neurobiological research into the developmental and integrative aspects of the central nervous system describes changes occurring in the brains of adults who were sexually abused in childhood (Bremner et al. 2003). Numerous other studies using scanning techniques have reported the negative impact on parts of the brain responsible for learning, memory, and processing emotions in those who have suffered child abuse. A recent paper by Fitzpatrick et al. (2010) cites a large number of research projects that support the belief that the effects of childhood abuse impact upon adult survivors in many adverse ways.

In summary, the long-term effects of childhood abuse are well documented by professionals and researchers. The emotional and physical trauma involved has an impact on mental health, relationships, intellectual development, and social functioning. It increases the likelihood of mental disorders, including post-traumatic stress disorder, depression, anxiety, dissociative identity and other psychotic disorders, insomnia, and agoraphobia. It increases the likelihood of diminished chances in life through education failure, unemployment, substance/alcohol addiction, self-harm, crime, homelessness, and the ongoing cycle of abuse. These problems destroy the lives of survivors and devastate relationships with friends, partners, and children. Survivors experience enduring social exclusion and disadvantage due to social stigma and denial surrounding child abuse. The effects are severe. Social exclusion prevents individuals and groups from participating and accessing opportunities in society and is frequently experienced by abuse survivors. They all too often feel alienated, scared, and different, which exacerbates further the impact of mental health problems so frequently experienced, often leading to social exclusion.

The need for specialist services

Ample evidence exists to highlight the benefits of counselling and support groups. For example, Coates states: 'assisting clients with histories of child abuse build supportive social relationships and networks is paramount to recovery' (2010: 399).

The need for services that provide longer-term help is critical. A research study carried out by the Department of Social Policy and Social Work at the University of York stated: 'more resources for free long term psychotherapy and counselling are needed', and that 'secure funding for voluntary organisations, especially for those that offer help lines and self-help groups for survivors of abuse, is needed' (University of York 1999: 34). The need for longer-term help is also summed up by the following words of a survivor:

> *I recognise that the NHS has limited resources but when dealing with chronic physical illness ... treatment continues while the patient needs it. It should be the same for survivors and particularly because they, if given appropriate support and allowed enough time, do become well.*
> (Department of Health 2006: 122)

More recent government initiatives aim to increase provision for mental health services (e.g. IAPT – Increasing Access to Psychological Therapies), and government campaigns to raise awareness of mental illness have helped. But this is often not the type of help that abuse survivors need and want. Most NHS treatments offer short-term interventions (often over six to eight sessions) based on a cognitive model. Many survivors carry with them such trauma from childhood that they can hardly begin to speak about what has happened in that short period – it takes time to build trust. They need a specialist approach specifically based on a thorough understanding of childhood trauma and its ongoing effects.

Our experience in Dorset has been that access to long-term counselling is rare. We have built good relationships with psychiatrists working in the health service and they recognize the need for our specialist services. Indeed, a large proportion of our referrals come from the NHS. Of course, long-term private counselling or psychotherapy is available and many of the experienced counsellors working for DAA have their own practices. However, the cost to a client is around £40–50 a session, beyond the reach of many survivors.

First steps

It was in the light of her own experience, and evidence of the kind set out above, that Moira Walker and a nurse-practitioner, qualified in mental health, paediatrics, and midwifery, together decided to form a group of interested people who wanted to explore issues and services for abuse survivors in Dorset. This resulted in an open meeting in January 2004 at Bournemouth University, where many people who were survivors, who were working with survivors, or who were interested in developing services for men and women survivors of childhood abuse in Dorset attended. Dorset Action on Abuse was born.

At this open meeting were representatives from many organizations, one of whom in particular was working with survivors and helped DAA to think about setting up our own organization. Gillian Finch was the founder of Cis'ters, an organization run by and for female incest survivors in Southampton. She shared her experience of how that organization had started, including her own story. This was useful and helped the fledgling group to formulate both what they wanted to emulate and what they wanted to do differently. For example, at that time Cis'ters worked only with survivors of incest, and was open only to female survivors. They had no professional input and were run on the basis of self-directed groups. Members of Cis'ters also presented their personal stories, which were very powerful. Their presentations highlighted the fact that abuse can and does happen anywhere and everywhere. Abuse is not confined to any particular social class, gender, ethnic origin, or level of financial security.

Those present at this event identified the following areas that needed to be addressed if a service were to be developed:

- Opportunities for networking that would foster making good referrals, especially for those with multiple problems and those on low incomes

- An ongoing professional group
- Sub-groups with specific interests, e.g. addictions, homelessness, primary care, resources
- Information about current services, a directory of services, a brochure that was also to be available electronically
- Mapping what was available and how survivors access these services
- Good-quality specialist supervision
- Training, noting the different levels of training that are needed
- Skills, knowledge exchange, developing skills, and widening experience
- Need for basic training, but also intensive training and skills development
- An academic interest group – the role of the university and university staff in taking this forward through inter-professional training and perspectives.

With the benefit of hindsight, these aims were too broad. We were perhaps over-ambitious in looking at what we could achieve. Looking back, a more useful way forward would have been to take each of these statements and set some reasonable objectives to work towards in each.

Dorset Action on Abuse was launched as an inter-professional agency/group for those working with or interested in working with, or who were already providing services for, men and women adult survivors of childhood abuse in Dorset. A core group was established with the following broad aims:

- To disseminate information
- To network across professions and voluntary groups
- To map service provision in the area
- To look at needs both met and unmet locally
- To explore possible ways of responding to these
- To work with survivors and others to develop services.

The core group welcomed anyone who was interested in actively developing the services for adult survivors, and one of its greatest strengths was its diversity, as well as enthusiasm. The original group included adult survivors, health professionals, social workers, Samaritans, and university academics.

There were adult survivors at the first open meeting who were eager to become involved in the development of DAA, and this inclusiveness became a central ethos of the organization. The core group wanted to ensure that there was no differentiation between survivors and professionals, and all decisions were made by a democratic vote of those present. This principle was held to throughout the life of the core group although, as we discuss below, there were some difficulties.

Creating a counselling service

Running in parallel with this initiative was an idea put forward by Moira Walker and Ann Daniel – another founder member – to develop a counselling service. Both had started to work at the Social Work Department of Bournemouth University early in 2003. They had known each other previously through their counselling work and immediately formed an alliance. They reflected on their past experiences of counselling and agreed that no matter what issue was presented by clients when seeking counselling help, there was often (although not always) an underlying element of childhood abuse. Both felt passionately that this area needed to be addressed. Adult survivors of childhood abuse may present in many of the ways described above. Moira's research, resulting in her book *Surviving Secrets* (1992), documenting case histories of adults who survived childhood abuse, was a testament to this. This knowledge fuelled their determination to set up a specialized counselling service in Dorset. In conjunction with Poole Mental

Health Social Services, and with support from Bournemouth University as part of its Community Outreach, they were successful in developing a service that provided:

- Free counselling sessions of fifty minutes per week

The need for the service to be free to clients was seen as fundamental to the belief that no one should be turned away because they could not pay. They saw the service as comparable to any health or social provision – free at the point of delivery.

- Weekly sessions for up to eighteen months.

The decision to offer up to eighteen months was an important standard, as both Moira and Ann knew that short-term counselling had limited success. It became one of the founding principles for DAA.

Potential clients and the Poole Community Mental Health Team (CMHT) were provided with written information about the process, as well as about the counsellors themselves, including their training qualifications and experience.

The service started with very limited availability (Monday and Wednesday mornings). This raised issues that occur at the beginning of any new venture: how and when to advertise the services on offer. It was important not to raise expectations unrealistically. Service users had described how they felt re-abused when this had happened to them. Some had been waiting for many months for counselling on the NHS, only to be told that they had only six sessions and that these would concentrate on the future. This demanded a very high commitment from the counsellors – there was to be no 'looking back'.

Initially, clients could access the service only after an assessment by the Poole CMHT. The counsellors were allowed a half-day each by the university to provide this service, and they each worked with three clients at any one time.

A number of working practices were established to ensure an ethical service.

- Clients were guaranteed confidentiality: Poole CMHT passed the client information to the counsellors, and there was an agreement that Poole would *not* receive feedback, other than any negotiated between counsellor and client. The counsellors both worked to the BACP Ethical Framework, which does provide for the breaking of confidentiality under very specific circumstances.
- Poole CMHT was informed only when the counselling ended, or if the client did not start the process.
- Poole provided rooms in a building that was multi-purpose. No client could be identified as receiving counselling when arriving or leaving the session.
- The counsellors underwent Criminal Records Bureau (CRB) (now the Disclosure & Barring Service or DRB) checks.
- They had regular peer supervision with each other in accordance with BACP requirements and consequently shared information about all six of their current clients.
- The counsellors never worked in the premises alone.

After a year

In March 2005, an inaugural day conference entitled 'From Hurting to Healing' was held to formally launch and celebrate the formation and first year of the work of DAA. Invitations were sent out to everyone who had a connection with the service, as well as to all the professional and voluntary organizations that might be supporting adult survivors of abuse. The pattern of the day included presentations from nationally renowned speakers with facilitated small group discussion groups to reflect on their input. These small groups enabled conference delegates to talk about the issues raised and to network. This was an essential feature of the day.

At the end of the day, Moira Walker closed the conference by listing the achievements made to date by DAA:

- An enthusiastic and committed core group representing a wide range of skills, experience, and interest had been formed to organize DAA
- A structure had been created whereby the core group met every six weeks to organize and plan
- Larger open meetings were held every three months, with visiting speakers and time for networking
- In collaboration with Poole Mental Health Services, a limited counselling service for women survivors had been set up
- Training events had been planned
- A constitution was being agreed, and application for charitable status was being actively considered.

First difficulties

The service provided by the counsellors to Poole CMHT continued for eighteen months, but ended when Moira was unavailable for a period of time; without peer supervision, Ann felt unsafe in her counselling practice. This, together with the reorganization of Poole CMHT, brought home how precarious the service was. With reluctance the counselling service was disbanded for a while.

In October 2007, a part-time professional psychotherapist was appointed to undertake restructuring and development of this service. In addition to undertaking all assessments and allocations of clients to voluntary counsellors, she was a part of the supervisors' group. Volunteer counsellors were recruited from colleges offering diploma-level counselling courses as well as fully qualified counsellors in the locality. They were required to belong to a professional organization, and to undertake support and supervision from that organization. They made a commitment of at least a year with DAA. Each counsellor was allocated three clients, and all were supervised by qualified volunteers.

However, there were significant issues at this stage. There were no suitable premises, and funds were fast running out. In addition to the counselling service, there was a self-help support group who had named themselves 'From Hurting to Healing'. It operated on the basis of weekly meetings with agreed ground rules. A professional supporter was a contact point, offering a confidential telephone debrief if required by individual members. She also visited the group every six weeks to review the ground rules with the group; issues around confidentiality, and the requirement that what was talked about in the group should not be discussed outside the meetings, were regular issues for review.

The group ran successfully for some time, but serious concerns arose as the group members experienced problems around maintaining confidentiality, as well as difficulties maintaining positive and constructive relationships. In analysing the failure of the group, it was recognized how vulnerable the group members were and that to expect them to take care of group processes, as well as supporting one another, was too big a task.

As our organization has developed, an experienced practitioner who can hold the boundaries facilitates all groups, allowing group members to focus on their personal issues.

Funding

For DAA to be able to access more substantial funds, it was clear that it needed to become a properly constituted charity. Charitable status was applied for and granted in 2007. This brought advantages and disadvantages. The core group of people who had given much time and input in an *ad hoc* but passionate and committed way was no longer fit for purpose.

Structures had to be adapted to comply with the Charity Commission. Trustees were required who would be responsible for the governance of the organization. Many members of the original group were prepared to become trustees, but this was difficult for some of the service users who did not feel able to take on the legal responsibility. Unfortunately, that led to the dilution of one of the founding principles, and for a while the trustees had no service user voice. However, several people already had experience of being a trustee and volunteering. This really helped the organization to navigate through the legal forest of Charity Commission requirements and financial propriety.

It was necessary to differentiate between the multiple tasks of the organization. Core group meetings had up to then discussed all issues concerned with counselling and the groups, as well as funding, training, and so on. This had raised boundary and confidentiality issues. The board of trustees, with different responsibilities for managing the counselling service, offered the opportunity for the necessary separation. The trustees are crucial for the proper running of the charity, and its legal and financial accountability. It was realized very early on that the organization needed to have people with financial knowledge and experience. Fortunately, a qualified and competent volunteer agreed to come in to manage the books, and a trustee with extensive financial knowledge became treasurer. Over time it has been necessary to broaden the diversity of the group, bringing in people who have different skill-sets. They may have little experience in counselling or working with survivors of abuse, but their skills in all those areas that ensure the smooth running of an organization are essential. This brought recognition from professional and statutory organizations as well as access to funding streams.

No organization can function without funds. Despite core group members and professional trainers and counsellors working on a voluntary basis, there were costs. Although these were kept to a minimum, advertising and room hire were unavoidable expenses. Some income was raised through training events, particularly the larger events and conferences.

This is a typical double bind that many charities find themselves in: no money, but with everyone a volunteer there is little time and few resources to raise money. It was decided to take a risk, and in 2006 a part-time fundraiser was appointed to apply for grants from local authorities and charitable trusts. This was a wise decision, and regular and substantial sums were raised this way. Inevitably, fundraising continues to be a core activity.

Even at this early stage, sustainable funding was needed in order to grow. It was decided to submit a bid to the BIG LOTTERY Community Fund. It was an ambitious request, because DAA needed both dedicated and secure premises, and someone to coordinate the growing service. In 2009 the bid was successful, resulting in five years of funding, starting in December 2010. Prior to receiving the grant, DAA was six weeks from closure! This was therefore the real launching point for DAA, and the start of the second stage of DAA's development.

Stage two

Premises were our first concern. A house was leased for five years at an affordable rent, providing four counselling rooms as well as an office, kitchen, and waiting area. It was on a bus route on a main road, not far from a train station, and with some car parking space. It was very important to create a safe and calm space that allowed survivors to feel supported and cared for. An interior design company donated its services, creating four different styles of room. John Lewis Partners gave a large grant to spend in store, providing comfortable chairs, cushions, curtains, and pictures to make the rooms welcoming. Many visitors have remarked on the tranquil atmosphere.

While we already had a part-time coordinator, Lottery funding enabled this to be made a full-time post. The service coordinator and the chair of trustees were the key developers. The amount of time taken to develop an organization that was working towards managing twenty counsellors, each with three clients, should not be underestimated. Having a full-time coordinator made an enormous difference to the consistency and continuity of the service. Nevertheless, the biggest oversight in the Lottery application was to underestimate the time needed for actual administration of the service. We budgeted for only eighteen hours a week of the coordinator's time – the rest being for assessment and clinical work. It was soon clear that this was woefully insufficient.

The opportunity to grow brought many challenges as well as delights. As the number of volunteer counsellors increased, systems had to be introduced to ensure ethical and safe practice, policies for contracting with the counsellors, assessment of clients, matching clients to counsellors, ongoing supervision, a complaints policy, record-keeping, safeguarding, equal opportunities, as well as financial accountability.

Dorset Action on Abuse becomes Hurting to Healing

In 2017, DAA changed its charitable status to Charitable Incorporated Organization, and after consulting with our service users and volunteers, we took this opportunity to change the name of the service to 'Hurting to Healing', a name that reflects our work and our beginnings. With our previous identity of DAA, many had expressed confusion about our mission. 'From Hurting to Healing' was the name given to our very first self-help group by the participants themselves. We hope that Hurting to Healing more clearly reflects the hopes and aims that our beneficiaries hold for their recovery.

The backbone of Hurting to Healing has continued to be the group of volunteer counsellors who give their time freely. Hurting to Healing is indebted to them for their commitment. Each applicant is interviewed to ascertain their potential to offer the specialist support needed for clients who are survivors of abuse. Many are trainees in their final year of study and do not have years of experience, but they are selected where it is clear they will be able to develop their skills. It is crucial that a counsellor can provide a 'safe pair of hands', is able to hold a safe space, and can create a supportive, caring relationship that can be sustained over a year. A minimum two-year commitment is asked of counsellors, though many stay longer. Hurting to Healing's commitment to them, and to offering a quality service to clients, is to provide specific specialist training and regular, professional supervision.

Each counsellor agrees to work for three hours, offering counselling to three clients. Every two weeks they meet with two other counsellors with an experienced supervisor for ninety minutes. In the intervening week there is always an experienced counsellor available for debrief, and someone at the end of a phone at other times to pick up queries or worries. Counsellors never work alone in the building. This level of support is crucial, as many clients are very vulnerable and present with very serious problems. There is also a supervisors' group that meets every six weeks, facilitated by an experienced psychotherapist, and Hurting to Healing has begun training some of its counsellors as supervisors.

Training and conferences

Based on the very successful inaugural day conference, the core group agreed to hold an annual conference to raise awareness and good practice, inviting speakers with specialized knowledge and national status. The target audience was defined as:

- Survivors of abuse
- Professionals working with potential service users in local voluntary organizations, particularly those working with addiction issues such as alcohol or drugs
- Social Services, NHS, and voluntary independent mental health organizations such as Rethink and the Richmond Fellowship
- Parenting groups, refuges, childcare facilities, etc.
- Professionals in training – social workers, nurses and midwives, counsellors, etc.

The conferences have a format that always includes presentations from survivors, who talk about their experiences of abuse and the subsequent effects in their adult life. Their experiences are compelling, often very raw and intensely personal, and they powerfully illustrate the reason for the need for Hurting to Healing. Those who support the survivors to tell their stories are immensely privileged and humbled. Feedback from conference members invariably highlights the input from survivors as both informative and emotionally challenging.

Other more local events are also organized. They have a dual purpose: to raise funds as well as to raise awareness and develop knowledge about the issues of surviving childhood abuse. They provide a means of networking within the area. Topics have included:

- Ways of dealing with disclosure of childhood abuse
- Possible triggers to identify childhood abuse
- Links between childhood abuse and suicidal thoughts
- Problems associated with parenthood
- Ways for professionals to avoid re-abusing survivors
- Self-harm and possible causes of it
- Legal processes when survivors have to give evidence.

Hurting to Healing today

The five-year Lottery funding enabled Hurting to Healing to grow and consolidate. However, there are constant funding issues, particularly in these austere times, when all charities are struggling to survive. The coordinator has become the full-time Service Director, who is responsible for the management of all day-to-day activities, including ensuring that all counselling-related activities meet professional standards. There is also a full-time administrator, as well as a part-time fundraiser. These posts are crucial to maintaining the level and standard of service required.

As part of reviewing funding, Hurting to Healing has been obliged to reconsider its policy of voluntary contributions for counselling. This has been a difficult decision to make, but an arrangement has been introduced, which involves discussion at the assessment session, concluding with a commitment to pay according to individual means. There is some flexibility to allow for changes and difficulties. This system is in its infancy but seems to be working well. Payment is seen as being part of the therapeutic working relationship, and is therefore an area of discussion between counsellor and client.

A group of Friends of Hurting to Healing has been created to provide a framework for those who want to support Hurting to Healing in an informal way. All ex-service users are invited to join, and there is an open invitation to anyone who comes across the work, either through the website or through personal contacts. The Friends have two main aims: to raise funds and to increase awareness of Hurting to Healing.

After ten years there is now a community of people committed to Hurting to Healing, offering a caring and supportive environment. Over this period of time, clients have received counselling, and their feedback and involvement have been essential for the development of the organization. There have been many challenges along the way, and much frustration, anxiety, and emotional upheaval as Hurting to Healing has grappled with the changes, opportunities, and losses of a developing organization. The chapters that follow show just what has been done, and what can be done to bring healing to those whose experiences growing up have been so damaging.

3

Survivors speak

Rosa Hubbard-Ford

> *An exploration of survivors' experiences and the impact of abuse, particularly with regard to helpful and unhelpful interventions • what do they need? • do they receive it? • where are the gaps? • what is the impact on families, children, and parenting? • is there sufficient recognition of the complexities and extent of the impact of abuse on the abused?*

This chapter shares the experiences of the brave survivors who want their stories told in order to help others, and to support the work of Hurting to Healing. Their narratives have many themes in common, although every victim of abuse has his or her own individual story. They each have tales of childhood trauma affecting their lives, sometimes memories not surfacing until later in life. They have all experienced great distress throughout their lives. And they show how their counselling at Hurting to Healing has given them a new and better life, a newfound sense of self.

Identifying details and facts have been altered to maintain confidentiality, but the stories are genuine accounts, and the extracts are taken directly from those accounts.

Excerpts from each of the stories provided have been used, so that each person has a voice and has made a contribution to the chapter. The first story, that of Audrey, is typical of many of the stories, in that people who feel they have had ordinary lives only come to realize later that they have been deeply affected by childhood abuse.

Audrey's story

Audrey, a trainee nurse, was feeling pleased with herself. Living in a nurses' home gave her a sense of being safe. It felt like being in a boarding school with friends who were always there for her – not the sense of isolation she had felt in her home as a child, where she felt no one had cared for her. Audrey greatly valued her nursing colleagues and the sense of security she experienced in the home, sensing she was not alone; being a nurse meant being part of a team, with people looking after one another. This was such a contrast compared with her childhood home life. Audrey had put all the abuse issues to the back of her mind; after all, they had happened when she was a child, so she did not think anyone would bother about that – even herself. Her only defence against the memories of childhood abuse was dissociation, although she did not realize this. She considered that she now had the best life and relationships she had ever experienced. Life seemed good.

As Audrey prepared for her first year's night duty, she checked herself in the long mirror on her wardrobe door before leaving her room. 'Yes,' she thought, 'I look pretty good and ready for this new exciting step in my career progression.' As befits someone dedicated to her nursing career, she was excited and smiling. Indeed, she looked smart, her uniform having been neatly pressed earlier that afternoon. Her hair was newly washed, brushed, and swept up and secured off her face. Her hands and short nails were immaculate, as was necessary for someone responsible for the health and hygiene of her vulnerable patients.

Audrey reported at the hospital for night duty, where she was assigned to look after men who had had a prostatectomy during the day. Procedures for looking after men who had had that kind of operation have obviously changed since then, but nevertheless her story encompasses much of the legacy of abuse – no matter how long a time has passed since it happened. If it is not dealt with appropriately, the traumas can resurface.

Audrey recounted that four of the patients were quite ill, because it was horrific surgery in those days. She said:

They all had catheters in their bladders that had got blocked up with clots and things. I had to attend to these people with the utmost vigilance and care throughout the night in case their catheters became blocked. If they did, then I'd have to hold the man's penis and just move it a little bit just to see if there was a clot sitting on the top of it that might shift or whatever. Or failing that I might have to pump some fluid through to disseminate clots, or whatnot. And it was then I was actually touching men's private parts that had been shaved. And I thought this is like the abuser's skin felt. He never had any hair on him. I never thought about it, but he'd obviously shaved himself prior to his encounters with me and he always looked a bit like a plucked turkey down below where he had so meticulously shaved every hair off from everywhere on his body. And now I was seeing these poor souls and touching them and it was like touching the abuser again. I suppose that was like a seed being sown in the brain that seriously, seriously was not quite right. And I was thinking, 'I don't care about that. It happened when I was a kid. Who bothers about that really?' I wasn't consciously bothering about it, but I certainly stopped sleeping again.

Later, after much conscientious work and dedication, Audrey passed her final exams, and was working in theatre, when people around her noticed she had become silent. She suspected this was because she had to work with male charge nurses, who were in the majority in the theatre, and she simply didn't really want to speak to men. She recalled that if they spoke to her, she would turn her head away. She often started crying and thought it was because she had been working very hard without a holiday. As a qualified member of staff, she went to see the matron and requested two weeks' holiday.

It was during this holiday that she found herself crying even more, and with suicidal ideation for the first time ever. Audrey went to see her doctor who put her on very strong medication to control her depression. She returned to the doctor as she found she had been tempted to take them all with a bottle of sherry. Subsequently, Audrey was sent to see a psychiatrist and was off work for about a year – a year away from her beloved career that had given her an identity, sense of self, and purpose in life. Audrey had not told the psychiatrist of her childhood abuse – she had pushed it to the back of her mind. She had thought the reasons for her feelings were other than that, such as working very hard in a stressful career, not that the abuse was central to her state of mind. Audrey eventually felt better, carried on with her life, and met a 'lovely man' whom she married, and to whom she was still married years later when she became a client at Hurting to Healing.

As can often happen with people who have suffered childhood sexual abuse, Audrey found marriage difficult. She enjoyed feeling loved, but subconsciously had not realized marriage would mean sexual intercourse. She had to drink alcohol in order to have sex with her husband, and did not like to be seen without clothes on. She thought she was just shy, not realizing the connection with her childhood sexual abuse.

Another awful moment was when a flashback occurred on her wedding night, when she smelt her husband's semen for the first time – and not wanting to hurt her husband, and not being able to verbalize anything about her childhood sexual abuse, she kept silent. They eventually had children and a good life looking after them. Once the children were old enough, Audrey went back to the work that had previously given her a sense of purpose and identity.

Everything seemed to be okay with Audrey's life, until one day she was passing the house where the abuse had occurred all those years before. There was another flashback, and feelings about what had happened in that house resurfaced in a big way. She decided to see a counsellor, but was offered three sessions only – and this did not do much good. Some years later she found herself with the blackness descending again. This time there was a change for the better, since she met a trainee counsellor from Hurting to Healing at her local church, who suggested she contact Hurting to Healing for some long-term counselling. Her previous counselling had seemed like applying 'sticking plasters' to her severe psychological wounds. Audrey was desperate for help and hoped that longer-term counselling might be available to her. Hurting to Healing indeed made all the difference – she was given a long period of time to explore and overcome her abuse, finding a voice herself, understanding herself and her reactions, and learning her abuse was not her fault. She had found a specialized service with excellent training, and time, commitment, and experience to help her overcome her abuse.

Seeking help

Hurting to Healing clients have suffered several forms of abuse – sexual, neglect, physical, and emotional abuse, including bullying; and of course all these types of abuse result in psychological abuse. Sexual abuse features in many of the stories of female clients, such as Audrey, as well as in the cases of all the male clients whom I interviewed for this chapter. Neglect, physical and emotional abuse, including bullying, feature in others. In the creative therapy group (see Chapter 5), four of whom were interviewed, the abuse was mainly psychological and emotional, so being in a group setting with others who could understand what they had been through helped enormously.

Audrey primarily suffered sexual abuse. So had Dennis, a seemingly successful businessman in his mid-fifties. Dennis had been abused by his parish priest when a young adolescent. As an adult, he sought help through his GP, but because the counsellor to whom he was referred had not had any specialized training in sexual abuse, the therapy did not help: she had in fact broken down in tears when hearing his story. He was then referred to an older male counsellor, who again had not had training in dealing with sexual abuse. Subsequently, he was referred to a psychiatrist. He described this as 'possibly the scariest thing I've ever been through in my life'. The whole onus of any treatment seemed to revolve around psychotropic drugs, which caused him to lose the ability to make any sort of decision about anything. Coming off medication did not help either, and he was lost in the slurry of despair.

Dennis wondered how it was possible to deal with the sexual abuse. Where could he go for help? His Achilles heel was worrying about what others might think of him if they knew his history. When he was a young adolescent, he had had to keep the abuse secret for fear of being an outcast from the church community, and this pattern of fearing that others might find out about what happened to him pervaded his adult life. He became paranoid about others guessing his 'secret', and how he had reacted to his abuse, and that he would be ostracized from society. Guilt, which should not belong to him but to the abuser, was his constant companion. Such a difficulty for someone brought up in a faith community where trust had been violated. Who could he trust? What a terribly lonely place for him to be! He was a very sensitive and troubled soul. A chance meeting with a voluntary counsellor from Hurting to Healing changed his life – he found an organization that could 'hold' and help him, where counsellors were trained to assist him in reclaiming his life so he could be free of the acting out that was part of the inheritance from his abusive past.

Dennis explained that 'just being able to talk to someone apart from his wife had helped him enormously'. He needed time to learn to trust his counsellor, to have his stories validated, and his feelings understood. Before coming to Hurting to Healing, others had told him to 'just get over it, it happened a long time ago!' At Hurting to Healing, he realized he had been one of the many vulnerable youngsters who had been abused by what he called

> *... the biggest crime [that] society doesn't want to deal with, society as a whole. Because it is embarrassing. We still live in a hugely male-dominated society. And men in power [can be] quite ruthless somehow. There are so many factors when you start talking about politicians and all these other weird secret societies and groups of people.*

He had experienced great difficulty dealing with emotions and closeness. Being listened to and believed in a setting where no one was judgemental was of immense help. Learning that he was not the only one to feel the way he had done all his life helped him to integrate back into society as a stronger man. Understandably, he had found it almost impossible to enact this recovery on his own.

Similarly, Harold, another male client, in his mid-forties, who was married with grown-up children, felt he could never trust people due to the sexual abuse he had suffered at the age of 10 by a well-known person. He had held that secret to himself for about thirty-five years, putting it to the back of his mind in order to cope – again dissociating from things with which he could not cope. The trigger for doing something about it was seeing the man's face in a national newspaper.

Invalidation

As children, most abused clients do not feel worthy and their stories are nullified. Sometimes they do not realize that they had been abused until they are much older – life as it was seems 'normal' to them. Ada, a 44-year-old housewife, told of being threatened that no one would believe her and that her mother would be killed if she said anything. Her feelings were confused – she loved her father but could not understand his abuse of her. Brenda, a 48-year-old mother of three children, had been labelled a drama queen as a child. Audrey had been told that it happened when she was a child, so 'who bothers about that?' Similarly, Dennis said:

> *If you introduce sexual abuse into social conversation, which can be quite a difficult thing to do, two things happen. One is that you get those people saying 'That happened thirty years ago, just get over it.' But also you get lots of other people saying 'Well it happened to me as well.' So many of them, who somewhere along the way have had someone take advantage of them. It's incredible.*

Khali, a 50-year-old mother and office worker, had suffered physical, psychological, and sexual abuse as a child. She recalled:

> *I think the thing at 8 years old, the thing I remember most when I was 8, is everybody else knew what was*

> *happening to me around me. My neighbours, but not one of them did anything about it.* [Sobbing] *That was what hurts the most. Your next-door neighbour knows that you're sleeping in the shed at night. My sisters and brother are asleep in the house. I was always afraid of the dark; I still am. I think that's just, you know, something that I'll always be frightened of – the dark.*

The abuse and pain experienced by this young child had been cruelly invalidated by those around her. The social workers assigned to the family had believed Khali's mother, and no one else had spoken up for her and validated what was happening to her.

Abuse has long been associated in the minds of the general public with sexual abuse, so Linda, a 42-year-old mother of three children, did not realize that the physical and emotional torment meted out by her parents, especially her father, was also abuse. She said:

> *I was determined [to] break some kind of cycle ... I didn't want to end up being like him. And even now when I find myself getting a bit cross or intolerant I'll think 'I don't want to be like him' ... But it's a difficult one, isn't it? Because I don't think anyone outside of the family kind of understands, you know, no one knows what goes on behind closed doors, do they? You'd always put on a great performance in public.*

How could anyone validate her story when she put on that 'great performance'?

Similarly, Olivia, a 67-year-old widow, had always felt 'I hadn't had a – I've always had a useless brain, told that I wasn't clever and I was slightly stupid and not intelligent.' She had felt so invalidated that she sensed she did not have any rights at all, even to breathe, and thought of herself as a bad person.

Isolation

Isolation was a pervasive theme in all our interviews. Some of this isolation came from feelings of shame. Ada had 'felt ashamed and dirty for decades'. Audrey said, 'I suppose that's what kept me out of my husband's bed. I felt like a person who'd got leprosy.' Lepers are isolated for fear of contaminating others, so her self-image made it hard to be around men, and thus her marriage and career were affected. Brenda typified some of those who had found that being isolated had helped them to cope. She stated, 'When I was a child I was very quiet, very withdrawn, terrified all the time of everything. Had always this sense of foreboding that everything was going to go wrong.' Dennis isolated himself because he feared not being believed, or was anxious about damaging his social life if he came forward with the truth. When he first came forward, he felt the police did not fully believe him. He lived in constant fear of judgement, and would isolate himself even more by staying at home and becoming a recluse.

Both Audrey and Marie, a 60-year-old married IT worker, used the word 'leper' to express how isolated they had felt. Marie, who greatly benefited from the creative therapy group, said in her interview, 'If you feel like a leper, it's best to be in a leper colony.'

Coping mechanisms

For some of the clients, coping mechanisms encompass ways of 'escaping' or running away from the situation, such as using alcohol and drugs, or having one-night stands. Brenda reported:

> *My drinking and my drug use became really, really bad. Everything on the outside looked great, but inside it was all falling apart. I couldn't hold down a proper*

relationship. I was terrified of any intimacy at all. I was having affairs with married men because they couldn't get too close to me. But I still felt like there was just something wrong with me. It couldn't be anything external. It was something wrong with me. Still very successful on the outside, I worked all the time. Completely work addicted and feeling like I was going to fail all the time... the pressure I put upon myself; perfectionistic, terribly perfectionistic, but at the same time completely powerless. It was just like a rollercoaster all the time. My self-harm, my drinking, my drug abuse, my eating disorder – all completely out of control.

Audrey could cope with sex only by drinking alcohol first to numb her feelings. As a devout Catholic, she attended daily Mass because the routine she found in Catholicism provided a good coping mechanism. Religion also meant a great deal to Elizabeth, a 61-year-old immigrant to Britain. She had been regularly beaten and ill-treated by her mother and stepmother, and sexually abused by more than one family member. She explained that, apart from the help from Hurting to Healing,

... the other person I need to thank from the bottom of my heart and is still always there for me is the Father Almighty. I am religious, I pray to [Him] for everything and He has never ever let me down. I've got Him to thank for never turning to drugs, alcohol, self-harming or anything like that. I think that is absolutely fantastic, that I managed to cope through, just through my belief in God.

Another coping mechanism for Freda, a 24-year-old survivor of neglect and rejection by her father and physical abuse on the part of her mother, was

... living behind a mask, I was made to feel that I'm young, I haven't got an opinion, I haven't got dreams

> *and things, it doesn't matter ... At school, as well, I think, because I was so quiet, I was silenced really. Being bullied as well, I didn't speak my mind at all. I just did the bare minimum in work and I got frustrated when I wasn't doing as good as I should do.*

Similarly Noreen, a divorced mother in her mid-forties, felt 'I just lived a life of pretend. I just had that mask and that's how I lived my life. Nobody knew me.'

Suicidal ideation was a major theme of concern as a coping mechanism. Audrey considered suicide but said she would not have attempted it. Elizabeth made suicide attempts at 14 and 19 years of age, and Dennis had considered suicide. He said 'he didn't care if he lived or died'. Khali had tried to overdose at the age of 17.

Other difficulties

Ada and Audrey both had difficulties that seemed common to many of the survivors – flashbacks and terrible nightmares, dissociation during sex, and the need to be in control.

Brenda believed it was her fault that she felt as she did. She was unable to cope with anger – either her own or that of others – and experienced great anxiety and panic attacks. She was unable to let her children have the freedom they needed as they grew up, since she could not trust other people, and never wanted them to be abused as she had been. Deirdre, a divorcee of 59 years, who was a mother and grandmother, and who had never been shown love and affection as a child, found her relationship with her children and grandchildren greatly affected. Her children were not

> *... touchy feely – because they never had it from me. They weren't cuddled and they weren't kissed like normal children. They were kept at arm's length. And they don't know why I did that, because I am very loving*

> *but can't show it. It's difficult to show. I think it's a lesson that was never learnt: how to do it with children. I just don't know how to. I find it very odd to even just cuddle my grandchildren. It's just weird. And I find it doesn't come natural. I mean, I didn't have a mum from a very early age because she was abused by my father as well, and she left us. She left when I was 9.*

Deirdre explained that she had had cognitive behavioural therapy (CBT):

> *But the GP services are just – I don't think they help anybody, because they're just too short. I've had counselling. I've had so much and it still hasn't done anything for me. I don't think the CBT helped at all. The counsellor just, well, she didn't come close to anything, just a waste of time. I just went because I was referred there and I didn't want to waste their time. But it was a waste of time. But here has been absolutely brilliant because I'm allowed to talk. I feel as though I've been listened to. And the more I talk the more I can sort things out in my head.*

Jackie, a member of the creative therapy group, is 57 years old, divorced, and a mother. She had been bullied at school and felt no one had liked her. She felt she 'didn't fit in'. She lacked courage and conviction, was unable to say 'no' when she needed to, and was full of anxiety and nerves. The creative therapy group helped her to mix with a few people. However, 'there were a couple there that I felt were – I didn't like; it's not that I didn't like . . . it's that we seemed not to get on. But I overcame that, which was good. Where before I wouldn't have been able to overcome it.' When asked how she had managed to overcome her difficulty, she said:

> *To overcome a difficulty like that, I put it in the back of my mind. Shut it away and stay away. But I did try to speak to the particular person. But it's strange,*

we never seemed to hit it off. It was a disappointment, but I think that's the way it went, but I learnt more that I could open up and give my own views than I would have before. I'm a very quiet person. Very withdrawn.

Later, she expounded on what happened to her:

It was with the face masks [which they made] and X [another group member] was absolutely petrified, and I mean throughout my life I've been petrified so much. And you go and you look at it and you think, 'Well before I joined Hurting to Healing I was the only one, there was no one there to help.' And to see someone going through what I've been through, it opened my eyes.

Not being the only one to feel the way she had, truly helped her to move on with her life and to communicate her feelings.

Gladys was our oldest interviewee at nearly 80 years of age. She came from a different era but was brave enough to confront her abuse. As a child, she had not been wanted by her mother. She knew her father had wanted her to be aborted, but then he idolized her – very mixed messages indeed. She remembered her mother saying, 'Who'd want to look at you?' and she constantly demeaned her. She had suffered depression, had two post-natal breakdowns, and been an inpatient in a psychiatric hospital at those times. She had been given electric shock therapy and told to try to overcome her painful life. Her childhood had been very lonely as she was never able to bring friends home after school because of her mother's attitude.

Recovery

Enabling clients to recover from their abuse has always been the objective of the work of Hurting to Healing.

What had helped, and what had not helped, our clients? Some of the answers to these questions are evident above, and the following summary is only a précis of our findings. It shows what enabled recovery, as well as what hindered their healing prior to them becoming involved in the work of Hurting to Healing. This is a further contribution to the evaluation of the counselling that Hurting to Healing has always conducted, assisting the organization in its development of ways to help survivors of abuse, but also serving as a template for other organizations and practitioners from various disciplines who want to build upon the experience and expertise of this particular agency.

All those who spoke to us for this chapter expressed gratitude to Hurting to Healing for many reasons. Here are some examples:

> *I now feel able to put my abusive childhood away into its proper place and feel able to move on with my life, it feels great to be in this place.*

> *I can socialize and go into open crowded spaces more easily and feel less panicky.*

> *I have a job after a long period of unemployment; my resilience and self-esteem have improved.*

> *I feel more in control of my life, more confident and worthy of having a good life and relationship. I believe that I am also a better parent.*

> *I'm not carrying the Burden of the Secret anymore. The abuser is no longer in my life. I don't live in fear and he is no longer controlling. My relationship with my daughters has improved.*

> *I no longer blame myself for past abuse or bad choices I made following the abuse.*

I'm seeing possibilities for the first time, I'm not living in a cave anymore, I'm okay to make mistakes, I can say no, I'm not living a half life. I have never had quality of life like this.

I am in touch with my grief for the first time in forty years. It is difficult, painful, distressing, but without Hurting to Healing it wouldn't have happened.

It has helped me to see that my defences were controlling my life, that by recognizing and accepting that the abuse was not my fault, I don't need to control those around me anymore. I can accept who I am – I have more freedom and so does my family.

There was consensus among many that they had needed more long-term counselling than had been available to them on the NHS or even privately. The dearth of appropriate help is due to a lack of resources, training, and understanding of what is needed. None of the clients had been able to access longer-term counselling until they had heard about or were referred to Hurting to Healing. Once at Hurting to Healing they had felt secure in knowing they were given the time they needed to unpack their stories, as doing so could be extremely traumatic, and could not and should not be hurried. It was important not to re-traumatize them, as many had been affected by flashbacks, nightmares, and physical and psychological manifestations of post-traumatic stress disorder. Short-term counselling or CBT had not been sufficient to effect the changes that needed to be made after years of carrying their 'secrets' of childhood abuse within themselves.

Although each individual interviewee had a different story to tell, they all shared their appreciation of the fact that Hurting to Healing offered a specialized service, with counsellors thoroughly trained in dealing with abuse. They also knew that those counsellors had ongoing training and were supported by experienced personnel within the organization. This gave them a sense of security they had not known before, since it was important to trust that whatever they revealed was accepted and validated by the counsellors.

While several of the survivors had been prescribed medication to allay their symptoms, this had not got to the root of their problems; but being 'held' in a safe and secure setting effected the deeper changes that they needed in order to move forward in their lives from hurting to healing. Some stated that in order to eradicate the pain they suffered, it was important to locate the primary causes of their various symptoms. Because of their training, the counsellors, of course, knew this and were able to work safely in collaboration with each client.

Some clients expressed gratitude for the strength they had felt, which enabled them to move away from people who influenced them negatively and from influences that had previously dragged them back into the victim mode.

In some instances, survivors' families had been affected by the traumas and symptoms of abuse, thus as survivors' lives were changed, so were the family dynamics. This had a knock-on effect, particularly on their children. Helping partners and parents to look at what they had brought into their relationships enabled a much more honest and healthy family system, which would hopefully make life better for future generations.

Many of the interviewees reported co-morbid conditions such as suicidal ideation, self-harming in the form of acting out sexually, addiction to alcohol and/or drugs, perfectionism, workaholism, and anger issues. All of these were as a result of childhood abuse. When childhood abuse was appropriately treated, these other conditions became less intense, with resultant benefit both to them as individuals and to society as a whole.

> **Conclusion**
>
> What our clients tell us is vitally important to them, but it is also important in a wider sense. Wider society has become more aware of the extent and ramifications of abuse since the exposure of abuse by some celebrities, and through the large number of people who have come forward with their stories of abuse. It is my hope, and the hope of Hurting to Healing's clients, that what they have told us, in their therapy and in this small piece of research, can make better known their experiences, both as children, and more positively as survivors seeking help, and that it will enhance the work of counsellors and other caring professionals.

Acknowledgement

The themes in this chapter were in the main identified by my colleague, Matthew Pittman, to whom I am immensely grateful for all his hard work and very sensitive contribution. I am also indebted to the valiant survivors for allowing me to share their stories. Their courage is a great example and testimony to the fact that, with the appropriate therapy, a shift from hurting to healing can indeed take place for each individual and their families.

4

The practitioner's experience

Jane Zoega

> The experience of counsellors working in the agency • the fragility of survivors in counselling • building up trust as a slower process • the centrality of the therapeutic relationship • a specialized field of counselling • the importance of time • identifying protective defences • dissociation • obstacles and barriers • stages in the therapeutic relationship • feeling connected • boundaries

Introduction

Drawing on interviews with five counsellors working at Hurting to Healing, current literature and published papers, this chapter explores their experience of forming therapeutic relationships with adult survivors of childhood abuse, and their interpretations of what they perceive to be happening in the therapeutic relationship. Their views offer insights into what to expect as a counsellor working in this setting. To ensure anonymity, no names are referred to and all the clients have been described as female even though some male clients were also discussed.

The interviews were semi-structured, with the focus on the counsellors' experiences of working with adult survivors of childhood abuse. Questions focused on all aspects of the therapeutic relationship – how a successful relationship is experienced, as well as obstacles and challenges practitioners faced. Despite the counsellors having very different levels of experience and different theoretical training, there were many similarities in how they perceived their clients and the therapeutic relationship. The counsellors interviewed were in agreement with other available literature and research, that working with adult survivors of childhood abuse is a specialist area of work, requiring a particular way of working in order to offer clients the best therapeutic experience possible.

In essence, humans are relational beings

It is widely accepted that survivors of childhood abuse have had their sense of safety, security, and basic trust shattered and as a result develop highly sophisticated and sometimes complex ways of surviving their childhood. These coping strategies, such as denial, dissociation, numbing, hypervigilance, and rejecting others, are developed to adapt to environmental surroundings, and in some cases to survive. The adaptive behaviours do not stop when the abuse stops, but continue into adulthood and adult relationships.

What emerges from these interviews is that counsellors perceive this client group to present as somehow more cautious and/or more fragile than other clients. Developing the therapeutic relationship is thus a slower process, but once trust has been established, the therapeutic relationship forms a pivotal part of the healing process for clients.

We are relational beings, we are born into relationships, we learn to define ourselves through relationships and, throughout our lives, our view of ourselves is especially influenced by relationships. We exist in relationship to ourselves, to others, and to the world. Buber wrote, 'In the beginning is the relation' (1996: 69), and 'the relation is reciprocity' (1996: 58). Relationships are nurturing, and give us a sense of safety and a sense of belonging in the world. On the other hand, relationships can also be hugely destructive. Criticism hurts when it comes from a person we are in relationship with, and abuse is particularly damaging when it comes from a person who is supposed to love us (Mearns and Cooper 2005). Human beings are social creatures; we thrive in healthy relationships. We have an innate ability to form relationships (Bowlby 1988), but we also have an innate drive to ensure survival. In order to ensure survival, we have ingenious ways of protecting ourselves from harm, both physical and psychological. In the case of repeated historical abuse within relationships, we adapt to our environmental surroundings by protecting ourselves from further emotional pain and abuse. Relational adaptations may result in individuals avoiding human relationships altogether or forming relationships where there is limited involvement. Others might develop self-protective behaviours where hypervigilance, or attacking before being attacked, becomes the perceived safest way to interact with others. The above examples are all potentially aspects of clients who wish to engage in therapy. A very common reason for clients coming for counselling is because of interpersonal difficulties, but there are particular difficulties in relating when people have been abused.

Many studies have shown that the quality of the therapeutic relationship makes a difference to the outcome of the therapeutic process (e.g. Yalom 1980; Bugental 1981; Cooper 2008; Krug 2009). Studies have also shown that adult survivors of childhood abuse have had their interpersonal skills damaged or compromised (Herman 1981; Kalsched 1996; Sinason 2002; Gerhardt 2004; Fisher 2005). Human beings are intrinsically embedded in the world, and we come to make sense of ourselves and others through our world dealings. Since we are always in the process of relating in one way or another, and since the way in which we relate depends on our experiences of the world, especially in the formative years, it is arguable that a compromised ability to relate will bring certain challenges for counsellors when working with adult survivors of childhood abuse.

The therapeutic relationship – part of the healing process

Many believe it is the therapeutic relationship that is the foundation for the treatment of adult survivors of abuse. By offering a corrective interpersonal experience, therapy allows access to reworking and integrating the traumatic material (Olio and Cornell 1993). Through the therapeutic process, emotional strategies can be slowly reworked over and over until eventually a new form of regulating emotional experiences becomes established.

Where there has never been trust, or where trust has been broken, difficulties arise when forming a relationship of any kind. According to Herman (1997), basic trust establishes a sense of safety in the world, and is acquired in earliest life in the relationship with the first caretaker, normally the mother. It forms the basis of *all* systems of relationships and, when shattered, life, the world, and others no longer feel safe. This is often the worldview of a survivor of childhood abuse. Similarly, Putnam (1997, cited in Fisher 2005: 24) finds that 'therapy with maltreated individuals is always concerned with trust and never moves very far from this basic issue'. Van der

Kolk and McFarlane (1996, cited in Fisher 2005: 24) add: 'the most powerful influence in overcoming the impact of psychological trauma seems to be the availability of a caregiver who can be blindly trusted when one's own resources are inadequate'.

Numerous writers and researchers continue to emphasize the importance of the quality of the therapeutic relationship as an indicator of the success of the therapeutic process. The counsellors who were interviewed for this chapter all seemed to be in agreement. When asked about the significance of the therapeutic relationship, one counsellor explained:

It is extremely significant. It is a huge part of the work itself. I see my own role as to maintain that relationship . . . because the damage is done in the relationship, I believe that is what heals them – the [therapeutic] relationship. I believe almost all the counsellor's work when dealing with abuse is based on the relationship.

Others agreed:

It's not so much about the model you use. It's about building trust in the therapeutic relationship.

It is absolutely essential. What I offer in a therapeutic relationship is an opportunity for clients to face themselves and face the issue, and I think it's unlike any other relationship they've had in their lives. I think there is no other relationship where they won't be judged; and that it's totally confidential and won't spill out, over into other relationships in their lives, family or work. I think the counselling relationship is very different to any other relationship, but I think with this client group, particularly, maybe it gives them an opportunity they have never had anywhere else.

All the counsellors similarly recognized that, for a person who struggles with relationships and who struggles with trust, making the commitment to having counselling is a very difficult decision. When it is a previous abusive relationship that has caused so much damage and pain, to enter into a new relationship involves both strength and courage. One of the counsellors shared her thoughts thus:

> *With this client group in particular, they have learnt not to trust people, and therefore they are being very brave in coming to counselling in the first place. To be just willing to put themselves in a position where they are potentially going to trust someone with this huge secret that they have hidden away. I have a real admiration for them. How they have lived their whole lives with this terrible beginning.*

A specialized field of counselling

Although clients are unique and differ in many ways, some similarities in how this client group presents emerged from the data gathered in the interviews. The counsellors all agreed that working with this client group differs to some extent from working with other client groups. As stated above, building a therapeutic relationship with an adult survivor of childhood abuse requires more time. The clients were described as 'fragile' and 'vulnerable', which led counsellors to describe their own approach as more cautious or tentative. With this in mind, it therefore seems prudent for those working with adult survivors of childhood abuse to be aware of what might arise when working in this setting. The following extracts describe some counsellors' experiences:

> *There is a difference; there is something more fragile about this client group. You have to be especially*

> *careful working and you have to be so sensitive to the needs of the clients and where they are and the pace that they need to go at. Going too fast can really slow things down, or taking steps back in terms of relationships. So it's very, very delicate work I find. Yes, I think delicate is the word that comes up for me more than any other.*
>
> *I've found differences. Yes, there is a big difference . . . because they take longer to connect . . . whereas other clients I've had are less tentative. I'd feel less inclined to take risks with, if you like, techniques and styles with this client group because I've seen the vulnerability in them, much more than other clients I've had.*
>
> *I am much more aware, because I feel it's my speciality, that when someone discloses abuse I am a little bit more tuned in, I know how to work with them, because I've been doing it for so long. I work very carefully.*

All the counsellors interviewed emphasized differences they had experienced, and many supported current published material about working with this client group. Valerie Sinason believes that survivors require a longer period of treatment. She also says, 'the slow and painful construction of the patient's narrative requires the patient to focus on the past while recognising the presence of the therapist in the here and now' (Sinason 2002: 61). The counsellors seemed to echo this belief. One said:

> *And I think that's why having longer contracts really works. It's not an easy thing to do, to form relationships, mainly because you're working with people whose formative relationships are characterized by abuse and neglect, and so trust is a very difficult thing to establish, and therefore the relationship can be difficult to establish because of those early experiences. Yes, they need more time.*

Another agreed: 'I think it is definitely long-term work. Trauma work takes a long time.'

Other differences that may relate to this client group were mentioned by one of the counsellors. She talked about the developmental impact abuse may have had on the clients:

> *Because of the sheer coping – they've had to spend so long coping with life that they haven't any emotions left to be self-reflective.*

This statement seems to support the views of Cloitre et al. (2006), who suggest that a traumatized childhood involves putting energies into strategies for maximizing physical and psychological survival at the cost of normal developmental goals of childhood and adolescence. A survivor of childhood abuse has almost always grown up in a family that has not provided the skills necessary for adequate functioning. In a good enough environment, these are skills that are taught and reinforced during the childhood years. There is limited published research in this area.

Identifying protective defences

Protective defences are behavioural adaptations developed in order to protect the self from further pain or abuse. These adaptations are often what maintain the client's compromised interpersonal experiences – protective defences that often protect the self keep others at bay. Several counsellors identified that working with adult survivors of childhood abuse highlights the ability of a survivor to hide what is really going on for them, especially emotionally. They wear their masks very well. This is an important point, because this is a well-rehearsed trait that can easily fool the novice counsellor. It is often worth gently exploring this a little further. The coping strategy of presenting as if all is well is often an adaptation developed from having emotional needs either ignored or even met with aggression or hostility, but the result of this adaptation can lead to feelings of loneliness. As one counsellor explained:

> *One of my clients presented as very happy and confident, but on further exploration, she told me this is what she does: when she says she is okay, she is not necessarily okay. She finds it very hard to present what she feels because she has spent her life 'being strong'. She explained to me that she doesn't want to be a victim.*

For this client, being happy and confident meant presenting to the world as not being a victim, whereas anything else felt like she was a victim, and therefore she was exposing herself to further abuse.

Many clients refer themselves to counselling because they have reached a point in their lives where something is not working; they often want to talk about what happened to them, but at the same time find it too hard to talk about it. Changing the subject, or talking about anything but the abuse, is another effective coping strategy for avoiding painful memories, yet remaining in a therapeutic relationship. Although it is important not to pressurize someone into talking about something when they are not ready to do so, the counsellor can gently explore this in the session. For example:

> *After a while I noticed that she would change the subject or make a joke about something. I fed back to her what I was noticing and asked her what that was about. It was really helpful, because she would then start to notice that about herself, and slowly, slowly, she would stop herself and either say she wasn't ready to talk about it, or she would open up about something she found hard to talk about. We would laugh about it at times. She said it was helpful. We had a really good therapeutic relationship.*

Other counsellors also describe how they perceive this incongruence between how the client is presenting and what is actually going on:

She presented as this quite 'together' professional woman. But on the inside she was so damaged.

They put a mask on. What you see is not what you get.

What is the most amazing thing for me is how the clients have survived to this point; and if you saw them walking down the road, you wouldn't even know they have problems. But yet they have such serious problems in making and maintaining relationships, and in everyday life.

One coping strategy, and an ingenious way of escaping psychological and/or physical pain when escape is impossible, is to dissociate. Dissociative disorder and dissociative identity disorder are new classifications in the most recent edition of the *Diagnostic and Statistical Manual of Mental Disorders*, DSM-5 (APA 2013). Dissociation is linked to childhood trauma and enables a child to escape unbearable pain when physical escape is impossible. Dissociation may become less helpful in adulthood, and can take unsuspecting counsellors by surprise. One counsellor shared her experience:

The other thing is the dissociation, so you are getting to know so many different parts. There might be two or three alter [egos] that need to be known, so you are working to connect with that one person, but their experience is of having several people [in them] and those might be different relationships; and [you come] to understand how they might use their bodies in any particular alter [ego] and [need to stay] attuned to that so you can respond accordingly. So it's not just responding to that one person I know, but it's

> *responding to that particular person in that particular frame, you know. I'm paying attention to their eyes, the way they might move their hands when they are in a particular alter, so you just need to be so alert and so attuned to what's going on all the time. Because if you say one thing that's fine for one alter but it may be not for the other. You have to think about the implication, so it makes it very complicated and that's why I think you need time as well because you need to really understand all of them and all their different needs.*

Some barriers to the therapeutic relationship

One way of protecting the self against further pain or abuse is to develop a psychological barrier to relationships with others. Relationships are dynamic and bi-directional. Client and counsellor affect each other, the relationship, and the space in between. Relational depth, a term used by Mearns and Cooper (2005), is a therapeutic relationship with a level of intimacy and connectedness that promotes relational healing. For this to occur, both parties need to be open to the therapeutic encounter. When interpersonal skills have been damaged or compromised, as they often have been with adult survivors of childhood abuse, there may be times when the *counsellor* is able to be open and present with the client, but the *client* is unable to relate openly and reciprocally. When asked to describe some of the difficulties experienced in forming a therapeutic relationship with this client group, and the effects of this, one counsellor explained:

> *Trying to find a connection with her and feeling like whatever I'm trying is not enough . . . but I don't know what would be enough. So it's like this vicious*

cycle really, for me thinking, what would be enough? And it's almost like I'm having a determination to connect with her, and I haven't found how to do it, and yes, that is frustrating and makes me doubt myself.

Many of the descriptions seemed to be based on feeling a lack of connection, or some form of detachment present in the relationship with some of the clients. Where relational depth was perceived to be lacking, counsellors seemed to find it hard to describe exactly what it was that was lacking. The existential philosopher Buber (1923) describes two different forms of relating, the I-it and the I-Thou forms. The I-Thou form of relating is a relationship without bounds, where individuals are fully available to the other, and the other reciprocates their availability. This is a relationship where both client and counsellor are available to the other and to the relationship itself. This is similar to how Mearns and Cooper (2005) describe relational depth. The I-it form of relating is a more objectified view of the other. Buber describes this as a way of relating where the other is encountered as an object to observe and learn about, rather than be in relationship with. Survivors have experienced trauma within one or many relationships and therefore may struggle to feel safe in relationships. A more detached form of relating may feel safer, thus minimizing the chances of further abuse and pain. Reinforced behaviour eventually becomes the norm, as detachment from others does indeed offer the desired result. Further abuse is minimized at the cost of relational depth. Counsellors, and arguably others in the clients' lives, may pick up this form of relating as detachment, a lack of connection or a barrier, as in the following example:

There was one client, from a different culture; it was very hard to form a therapeutic relationship with her. She just said, 'I feel better for telling you', but it was still very hard. Was it the culture? I think it was her, she'd been brought up not to say anything, and brought up to just get on with life; and if you've been abused, you just get on with it. And it was very hard, because I didn't want to pry too much, or probe too much, but yes . . . it was very hard to form a therapeutic alliance with her. She was very polite, very formal: 'It has been good to talk about it', and so on.

Other counsellors said:

I find it very difficult, because I am offering the same environment that I am offering the other clients, but she remains detached. She talks the talk, but it is almost like there is no emotion, no real emotional connection. I find it challenging; I don't feel I have a link with her, and I am trying to look at different ways of trying to get her round, but it is recognizing that it has to be her time, and she's not ready. But it is challenging. I like to feel a connection with clients; it feels like hard work for me.

Interestingly, this is also a client that I am really, really, very fond of, which is interesting because it took quite a long time to establish a relationship as well. And it was an interesting one, because the client would come to therapy and share everything. It wasn't that she didn't share, or that she would hold back, but actually she was sharing everything in detail with no problem – but there was no sense of there being something between us, which was preventing a connection and I found it really difficult to put my finger on. And again, I took that to supervision a lot because there was a time when it was quite frustrating, because I was thinking 'I can't tell you why this isn't good, but something is missing' . . . You can't put it into words, when you know it's there and I felt it wasn't there. And she shared everything, but I had this distinct sense that 'This is all the stuff, but [I] don't say anything. It's almost as if I am going to say all of this stuff but I don't want you to participate in it. I just want to say it and leave.'

Another counsellor described how this way of relating permeated into other relationships outside of the therapeutic encounter:

I found it hard to feel a connection with her. I really liked her, but she would talk a lot, filling the session with her talking, and it felt like she was keeping me at arm's length all of the time. She was aware that this was her way of relating to others. She told me she even keeps her children at arm's length, because she was scared of getting hurt when they grow up and leave home.

Other obstacles that counsellors experienced and described were clients presenting as helpless, passive, ambivalent about counselling, not attending and, on occasion, angry, all played out in the therapeutic encounter. When faced with challenging clients, there was an understanding that although difficult at times, this is part of the adaptive and self-protective behaviour that survivors engage in, in order to maintain a level of safety with others. Kalsched (1996) talks about the psychic split, where in order to survive, the child dissociates part of the self that cannot be integrated and, as a result, there exists side by side a vulnerable innocent part and a tyrannical protector. The survivor oscillates between the two parts, sometimes presenting as hostile and rejecting, and at other times as dependent and vulnerable. The way this might be played out in the therapeutic encounter is seen in the following quote:

The more I showed understanding, the more defensive and angry she became. And I found it extremely challenging. I think she was very uncomfortable about being in the counselling relationship. Looking back now, it is interesting that she came every single week. She came here telling me she doesn't like the way I work; she doesn't think this is working but she was here every week. Some weeks I dreaded coming in, but in the end we had a satisfactory ending.

With another client and counsellor, a very different coping strategy had developed in response to relating to others, as seen here:

One of my clients found it particularly very difficult to talk. It was quite difficult. I think she was very self-conscious, and didn't want to take up too much space in the room. I don't know how many weeks it took, but at first she didn't do much talking at all; but she gradually began telling her story, and that was very rewarding.

Stages of development in the therapeutic relationship

Counsellors experienced several stages in the therapeutic process. In the beginning, they described the relationship as a time when the client was testing the relationship and testing the counsellor, something akin to a pre-therapy stage. As one counsellor put it:

It feels like clients here are putting themselves in the position of being clients, but they're actually not sure about it. I would say clients here are tentative. It's taken a lot to get as far as the counselling appointment, and I get the feeling they want to talk about their abuse, but at the same time they are not sure they want to talk about it. They might talk about other things going on for them, or how the abuse has affected their relationships or their lives in general, but the actual abuse they can't talk about.

And another:

If they have been abused they haven't learned how to trust, or their trust has been broken, so sometimes you have to work for quite a while. Sometimes I'll have a client who might be with me for six months before they disclose abuse. In the beginning they are testing out, seeing how they can trust you with their innermost secrets. Building up trust takes time, it can't be forced, so they might go around it in different ways. They might bring all kinds of different things to you first of all.

When exploring the experience of forming therapeutic relationships with adult survivors of childhood abuse, there were several more comments that suggested there was something like a pre-therapy stage before that of relational depth, or an I-Thou way of relating. This appears to be a period where decisions are made about whether or not the counsellor can be trusted, or whether the counsellor is able to handle listening to their abuse histories. Counsellors described this stage using terms such as 'testing out', 'seeing if they can trust you', and 'they're not talking about the abuse, they're talking about something else, but they need that'.

Or, as one of the clients said to her counsellor, 'How can you listen to it?' This may be a time when clients need to have the opportunity to oscillate between the polarities of either accepting the relationship or rejecting it, a time to 'test the water', before taking a leap of faith into a new way of relating. As one counsellor explained:

The significant people in their lives have not been people they can trust, who can give them what they need, so they've learnt to shut people out. And to let me in, it's almost as if they are testing the ground, testing

> me: 'Is she going to be like all the other people in my life who have let me down?' A bit of testing process going on. And I'm offering them the opportunity to have a relationship unlike any other relationship they may have had previously.

Feeling therapeutically connected

When the counsellors described their experience of feeling connected to their clients, they all found it difficult to articulate exactly what that experience was like. A common theme that emerged when the interviews were analysed might be called a 'leap of faith'. This seemed to be a significant moment in the therapeutic process, the moment when the counsellor experienced a connection with the client, and when her perception was that the client experienced the same connection. London (1999) writes in an unpublished paper of the 'Wow! Moment', describing it as a significant 'moment of meeting that is very moving and special' (cited in Sinason 2002: 99). The experience may be mainly non-verbal – the result of a build-up of the relationship. When the moment is reached, the client and therapist are able to see it, experience it, to stand back and realize it and acknowledge it. 'Leap of faith' is a term commonly attributed to the Danish philosopher Sören Kierkegaard, meaning a transition from one existential position to another, from having no faith, to having faith (Kierkegaard 1844). In the case of counselling and the therapeutic relationship, it is the move from being detached and testing the relationship, to engaging fully in the therapeutic relationship openly and willingly.

The counsellors described this experience in various ways:

> She was telling me about this horrific abuse she had gone through. This was many years ago. She stopped

after a while and said, 'How can you listen to this?' She had tears coming down her face. I explained that I have been trained to help, trained to work with her mind. She relaxed at that point. She was a long-term client. A lovely person, with a terrible childhood.

There was a definite shift in our relationship. She used to sit on the edge of her chair, and she was really, really nervous and very stressed. But the shift took place, I remember, when she realized that she was actually in a relationship with me. I think it took her a few months, and when she realized that I am here with her, she started sitting back more into her chair. In the first few months she was there talking to me as if she was in her own world, and then the day came when she realized I am actually here, and that we were connecting.

I had this client, I liked her anyway, and I think I'd been feeling I desperately wanted to reach her . . . I felt at that point almost like I was throwing her the rope of a lifeline. And at that point she caught the other end. It was a long rope, but that was the point where I felt there was hope, that I could help her get what she needed, to tow her in, if you like. But with that connection there was almost a warmth, an emotional warmth that hadn't been there. Up until that point there had been a detachedness, but at that point it felt like a bit of emotion.

There is also an emotional response between the counsellor and the client when there is a feeling of connection: a sense of being in the moment. One counsellor described this as being like

. . . when someone can just be themselves, when they fall to pieces in front of you if they need to, and they know you'll be there to help them put themselves together again . . . it's very hard to describe, but you just feel it.

Another said:

> *I had this one client, a young lady, she was telling me about a rape, a terrible story. I shed a few tears when she was telling me. I didn't realize I was, but it was the fact that she said 'You believe me, you know what I am feeling', that really helped her.*

In one study, Mick Cooper (2005) explores the importance of the quality of the therapeutic relationship in determining the outcome of the therapy. He explores how therapists experience a sense of deep connectedness with their clients, similar to Csikszentmihalyi's (2009) description of the 'flow'. This is a state in which people are so involved in an activity that nothing else seems to matter. It is identical to the feeling of being 'in the zone' or 'in the groove', as in the example above, where the counsellor was caught in the moment, not altogether aware of what was going on for her.

When describing this sense of connection with a client, much of it is expressed non-verbally. Such significant moments are difficult to describe. Here is how three counsellors tried:

> *We just look at each other and know it is there.*
>
> *At that point it felt like a bit of emotion.*
>
> *I know that to say you feel it is not a very good answer, but there is just this sense of your client trusting you.*

Geller and Greenberg (2002) also found that when this presence was experienced in the therapeutic encounter, it was often felt as a moment of immersion and absorption in the present, a sense of timelessness, a sense of being highly receptive, and a strong feeling of 'being with'. Again the findings of this study seem to support the idea of something happening in the space between that our counsellors describe.

Boundaries and the therapeutic space

The counsellors all touched on the importance of considering the therapeutic space and boundaries when working with this client group. Where there is a history of abuse, the child has often grown up in a 'chaotic, depriving milieu of inadequate, distorted caregiving' (Steele 1990: 32). Clients are therefore not necessarily familiar with healthy boundaries and often do not have their own boundaries in place. It is important to remember that although relational depth is generally the aim in the therapeutic relationship, there is still a place for keeping safety in mind. As one of the counsellors explained, when asked about what she is mindful of when working with this client group:

Be very careful with keeping your own boundaries ... Boundaries are really, really important to keep. I had a female client once who expressed strong feelings towards me. I was very careful with how I dealt with her. I was careful not to reject her, whilst at the same time I didn't go towards her either.

Describing the significance of the therapeutic space, another said:

I had a client who I saw in a different room one week. She was really bothered by the change in room. It stayed with her all week and we were able to talk about it the following week. She didn't feel as safe in a new room, and she was rattled by it for a whole week, until she came back, we discussed it, and we were back in the usual room. I had no idea it bothered her so much.

Conclusion

What emerges from these interviews are the similarities that are experienced by counsellors despite the differences in their theoretical training and practical experience. They all agree that working with adult survivors of childhood abuse can be challenging at times, but there is also an immense sense of admiration and respect for this client group. Despite adverse childhood experiences, the innate instinct we have to endure drives these clients to develop ingenious and imaginative coping strategies that allow them to survive their childhood. Those coping strategies may become less helpful in adulthood and in adult relationships but, through taking a risk to form a trusting therapeutic relationship, clients are willing to make changes in order to have more fulfilling relationships and more fulfilling lives. As one counsellor put it:

> *I have so much respect for the clients here, for what they have been through, and how they are able to keep going. They have been through so much. They've had this terrible beginning, but you would never know, unless they choose to tell you that part.*

The findings in this study have highlighted some of the obstacles and challenges counsellors face when working with this client group, such as detachment, dissociation, anger, and lack of trust. What emerges is the perception that there is a stage prior to feeling connected in the therapeutic relationship, or what we might call relational depth, which feels like a stage of testing the relationship, or a pre-therapy stage. This is a time when clients oscillate between wanting the relationship but at the same time rejecting it, by criticizing how the counsellor works, by not attending regularly or by remaining detached from the relationship. The interviews also found that there comes a time when a shift occurs in the relationship, when clients feel safe enough to engage more fully. The counsellors found this difficult to verbalize, but they did describe the feelings of what connectedness was like. They just 'feel' it is there. I have called this shift in the relationship a 'leap of faith', a sense that the client has taken a leap into the unknown and is prepared to engage fully and openly in the therapeutic relationship. When both client and counsellor are available and open to fully engage in the relationship, healing can take place. Where the original damage was done within a relationship, a trusting therapeutic relationship can also provide the platform for repairing damage and building trust in order to learn to relate to others. Human connectedness and relationships are psychologically healing.

The Hurting to Healing counsellors were all in agreement that working with this client group is rewarding. They all praised the courage, tenacity, and resilience of adult survivors of childhood abuse.

However, it is challenging.

5

Working creatively with groups

Zoë Pool

> The particular value of creative therapies • selecting participants • creating a safe environment • examples of therapeutic arts processes • challenges to the process • participants' reflections on participation in creative groups

Expressive arts in therapy

All therapeutic models of mind–body therapies have explicit or implicit intentions for the work, rooted in the theoretical tenets and principles of practice of particular approaches. The relationships between two or more people in an agreed context, and what happens there, are two of the shared factors. Hurting to Healing's creative therapies take place within a boundaried, therapeutic group through an evolving process, starting from the premise that in myriad ways we are all creative. Time-limited, structured group sessions are offered over a set number of weeks, in a safe *enough*, contained therapeutic space, with opportunities to engage with diverse creative media.

The aim in this creative therapeutic approach is aesthetic rather than clinical, in the sense of perceiving, feeling, and sensing. Our intention is not to 'treat' or cure symptoms or disorders, but to promote awareness, welcoming rather than pathologizing connecting and fragmenting patterns of being (Gilligan 1997). In other contexts, where traditional, clinical or interpretative mindsets prevail, or where the emphasis is only on talking as therapy, these patterns, fragments, gestures, and 'half-formed articulations' (Smail 2013: 76) may be barely perceptible and may be discounted or go unnoticed. We ask, 'What do I see? Hear? Perceive? Sense? What is the dynamic between connections, fragments and disconnections? Moment by moment, who or what is alive here – in the self/selves or parts of selves in body and soul, soma and psyche? Who or what is emerging here and now, in the different dimensions of being? Who or what could gain from creative expression?'

Attempts to survive abuse may leave people feeling trapped, confused, and isolated, in situations that devour their freedom to feel fully alive. For many, the ability to use dissociative phenomena as creative tools helps develop a safe haven that enables survival. A trauma silenced, forgotten or unexpressed lives on, buried alive in the body. van der Kolk writes:

> *Trauma victims cannot recover until they become familiar with and befriend the sensations in their bodies. Being frightened means that you live in a body that is always on guard. Angry people live in angry bodies. The bodies of child-abuse victims are tense and defensive until they find a way to relax and feel safe. In order to change, people need to become aware of their sensations and the way that their bodies*

interact with the world around them. Physical self-awareness is the first step in releasing the tyranny of the past.

(van der Kolk 2014: 100–1)

For some, the telling and retelling of traumatic experiences through words alone is inadequate to heal childhood wounds. The thought of making such experiences explicit may strike terror into a survivor who has been told of the dire consequences of revealing atrocities done to them, and causes additional distress for some (see Figure 5.1):

In the beginning was abuse
Bad early attachment
Muzzled secrets.
I belong to no one.
I belong nowhere.
Aborted broken
The light poured out of me.
In the beginning was her word
and her word was law.
Ugly, dirty, good for nothing.
I brought you into this world
I can also take you out.
Today, the daughter knew why she had been fighting
   against the mother.
It was for her own sense of self
Her freedom to be.

Some survivors have found that although talking therapies help to an extent, their suffering is beyond words. Others find that describing what was done to them triggers unbearable sensations of violation. Carrying withered meanings in their bodies, frozen in time, survivors may be unaware that parts of themselves remain incarcerated. They may be unaware that they perpetually anticipate further

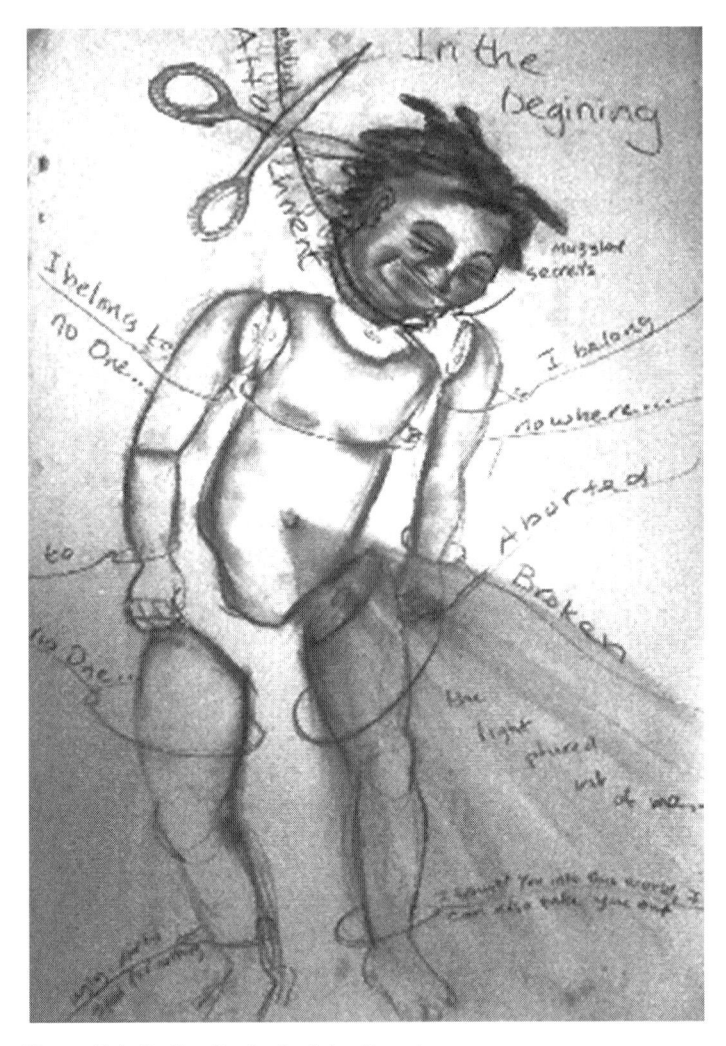

Figure 5.1 'In the Beginning', by Brenda

abuse: feeling, hearing, seeing or imagining threats, even if not intended by others.

The feminist philosopher Luce Irigaray exhorts women to connect with embodied possibilities for creating a language for self-expression: 'If we don't invent a language, if we don't find our body's language, its gestures will be too few to accompany our story. When we become tired of the same ones, we'll keep our desires secret, unrealised' (1985: 69–70).

As participants accept the invitation to connect with and express what is real for them, physically, imaginatively, emotionally, ideally/spiritually, their experience is empathically witnessed and reflected within the group. They are frightened, angry, stuck, struggling, and fed up with recurring patterns of destructive behaviour. The cyclical process of noticing patterns, of breathing and acknowledging, and empathically accepting what is within them, allows possibilities for liberation from rigidity.

A survivor, who had been physically and emotionally tormented throughout her childhood by a violent, psychotic parent, struggled with her right to be alive. The ideas of freedom and choice seemed out of reach. Expecting that any attempt at self-expression would be shaming, her belief in her creativity was crushed. She had survived the trauma of being unloved and violated, but struggled to overcome the wounds that cut deep grooves in her being. But in response to the questions 'What are you aware of? What might be a risk for you here? What is alive for you now?', she wrote:

> *I talk and talk*
> *You wanted me dead*
> *It nearly happened – try harder*
> *Your cruel words*
> *Still bruise my head*
> *Worse than the blows – try harder*
> *Look on the bright side*
> *It could have been worse*
> *It's time to move on – try harder*
> *Let go of the past*
> *Again I'm to blame*
> *I'm stuck in struggle – try harder*

*Each push forward
Every cut back
Again and in shame – try harder
The Memories choke
The past that haunts
The Cell with no door – try harder*

We cannot change the past or eradicate memory. Rigid frames of understanding can be buried so deeply that we are unaware of how much they influence us. We encourage movement towards acceptance of what cannot be changed. We welcome individual experience and difference. This allows for possibilities for what was fragmented to be accepted as unifying threads *within relationships*. We aim to give survivors a different experience of the present. 'Trauma treatment shouldn't have to hurt too much' (Fisher 2014).

Survivors may begin to feel safe enough to shift from a sense of being 'buried half-dead' to increased vibrancy, where they can create their own order out of chaos. Therapeutic, expressive arts can be transformative. Evaluating her experience, Lily wrote:

*Child abused – emotional,
physical, financial, sexual abuse
Steals your very soul, your spirit.
Buried years in a deep dark hell hole,
no light, no colour, no hope, no life.
Robs your life of colour and joy
awe and wonder.
Therapy should not all be about talking
taking you through
the blackness and darkness.
(Medication will never do this).
Therapy must also be about bringing into the
    darkness
Colour and light.
In each of us is a tiny core of hope
that needs to be ignited*

Fed and allowed to flourish and grow.
Our souls and spirit crave for this.
Find that. Feed that. Feed the soul.
We cannot do this on our own.
We need you to help us dig deep inside ourselves
To find this spark, ignite it and keep it fed
So it overcomes the darkness.
Creativity is the way to do this.
This multimedia creative therapies programme has brought me out of this darkness, into the light.
It has been brilliant! Life saving.

Selecting participants

A brief description of what is offered in the creative therapies' programme is available to prospective participants:

> *We invite you to participate in a creative journey of recovery and self-discovery through Movement, Meditations, Dance, Storytelling, Poetry, Drama, Music, Voice, Art, Film*

- Develop ways to focus, relax and heal in body-mind-emotions.
- Develop your imagination, increase your sense of purpose and well being.
- Build confidence and trust being with yourself and others.
- Feel empowered to move creatively and bring about desired changes in your life.

Our initial information for applicants asks:

- Are you a female survivor of any form of childhood abuse or neglect?
- Have you already had at least 6 months therapy or counselling to help you with your childhood abuse issues?

- Would you find it helpful to express feelings, ideas and experiences in a variety of creative ways?
- Are you ready to develop, express and share your creativity with others?

We meet prospective participants individually and assess their suitability and readiness to join the group. We liaise with external referrers when appropriate. Participants need to be stable and confident *enough* to be able to join with others, to feel contained in a group setting, to attend regularly, and to be willing to take part in expressive arts therapies activities (Meekums 2000). They should have some support in their day-to-day life, and/or access to additional professional support if necessary.

Group members may have completed or still be in counselling or therapy. Survivors present complex therapeutic needs, and can benefit from creative group work concurrent with individual therapy. We also offer participants contact with facilitators between sessions if additional support is needed.

Some clients referred to our creative therapies programmes carry a mental health diagnosis. Dissociative phenomena are frequent in our clients, although diagnoses of dissociative disorders remain rare. Some survivors of childhood abuse, but not all, find diagnostic labels helpful. Even in severe cases of dissociation, where long-term interventions are needed, individuals can benefit greatly from the holistic, body-mind-emotions-spirit approach found in expressive arts therapies. We work with the person, not the diagnosis or label.

Creating a safe environment

Prospective participants tell us they seek creative group work to experience connection with other survivors similarly drawn to this approach to self-expression. Even so, survivors may feel uncertain about the presence and connection with others, who may evoke unforeseen memories and emotions. Being present in a group involves risk. Thus, the essential foundation for our group work is a structure that contains – and prioritizes – safety, trust-building, and choice for every member. We seek to create an inclusive and non-judgemental environment. Mutually agreed ground rules and boundaries are established, and this group agreement is negotiated and revisited when necessary. Participants agree that if they experience conflict with another participant, or disquiet or confusion within the group, they will raise it within the group. This is easier said than done. Many survivors find it hard, if not impossible, to express their feelings or perceptions when confronted with any hint of conflict or power issues with others in the group.

Historical patterns of relating, connecting, and distancing are often re-enacted. One member reported:

Part of me that agreed to the ground rules thought I'd be okay speaking up, but when K went off on one, another part of me felt silenced. I couldn't say anything. As soon as she started it was like being a small child again, and she was my father, ranting. I remember I just shut off. It's like I felt something terrible would happen. I'd be judged or shamed, criticized I guess. I felt choked. I was glad you said something in the group and I could see she didn't like it. I didn't want to come to the next session, in case there was a show down. I know that would be a cop out.

What might constitute safety and trust differs from person to person (Figure 5.2). We encourage participants to reflect upon and share what safety means to each one of them and to be open to a possible change in what 'safe' means to them. We articulate the need for respect and safety, while recognizing blocks and difficulties.

Figure 5.2 'My Safe Place', by Hannah

Structures

As the groups have evolved, we have reduced the duration of each group from sixteen weeks of two-hour sessions, to twelve weeks of three-hour sessions. Reducing the number of weeks has made it easier for participants to commit to full attendance, and the longer session, with a comfort break, allows deeper work to take place. Each programme has a different focus or theme, so participants can apply to join a future group if they wish. Each session involves the following.

- Welcome: gather in circle, invitations to embark on a journey.
- Warm-up/ice breakers – breathe – stretch – move (relaxation, movement meditation, visualization, shake out).
- Transition into '*as if*...' We cross metaphorical bridges – symbolic connections.
- Creative invitations: Theme – Focus: art forms/creative media processes (dance, storytelling, poetry, art, drama, music, voice, film).
- Express – share – empathic witness – reflect.
- Return – grounding closure – departure.

This shape provides a secure enough base. We create a safe, transitional space, within a potentially healing circle (Smail 2013). We give every participant a sketch book/journal to use week by week. Everyone is asked to bring a small blanket and a cushion. Participants tend to make themselves comfortable in the same place every week – a spot that becomes their own safe haven. This space is separate from habitual everyday activities – a shared, imaginary space where healing work may take place. Our therapy dog sometimes joins us in sessions, encouraging healing connections with the animal kingdom. Gathered together around the edges of this healing circle, we might safely enter into a liminal realm, where in surprising ways we can discover beneficial possibilities to meet both ourselves and others with compassion and acceptance. Once gathered together, centred in breath, pulse, and the rhythms of life, we begin with an 'ice breaker'. From the circle, we venture outwards into creative territory, and return together for shared reflections and closure at the end of every session. The circle creates a sense of familiarity, a resting place, from which we venture forth.

Around the studio are ample supplies of art materials. In a quiet corner are two rows of empty, 'I need time out' chairs with soft toys sitting on them. I welcome the group gently: 'Metaphors be with you.' Making eye contact around the group, I open with a short, ambiguous poem:

just imagine now . . .
imagine . . . it's as if . . .
in between our words and thoughts
pictures dancing poems . . .
what if?
as if before. . .
between our breath in words
being always started here
what was sleeping now awakens . . .
our bodies – alive
breathe silent music
move through symbol
dance between words
to welcome the unsaid

I pause and then repeat the words, shifting the order of lines, the emphases, shifting pauses between the words and phrases. We then invite everyone to creatively 'check in'. Each member can express how she is in the moment – symbolically, through sound, spoken or otherwise with gesture or movement. We are entering a healing, embodied yet metaphorical realm, which offers an opportunity for authentic expression, but without explicit revelation. Much can be revealed safely in this way – or not. After another pause, the assistant facilitator says, 'I'd like to invite you now to each take a turn to say your name, and to express how you are right now, what is alive for you, with a gesture and a reference to an animal.' (Other metaphorical expressions include the weather, plants or trees, type of food or drink, modes of transport, characters from favourite book or film, sport, luggage, shoes or clothing.)

An example might be, 'My name is Psyche, and right now I feel like a cat that has just woken up and I need to yawn and stretch all my limbs.' We repeat each contribution together, twice.

One participant, who always struggled to express anger, swirled her arms energetically above her head and shared how she was feeling. 'Right now, I feel like a dark tornado, that swirls ferociously with an immense force across the landscape, felling trees and drenching the land.' When the group repeated her words and gestures with the same emphasis, her expression grew stronger and louder with each repetition.

Carefully selected expressive arts activities are focused towards what is going on for the group or for individuals, and can help participants to stabilize within the group. All aspects of each person are welcome within the limits of the group agreement and ground rules. We connect with our selves and with each other through metaphor, rhythm, gesture, movement, sound, pictures, poems, and stories. We invite expression of the multiple-relational, physical, imaginative, and emotional, remembering that below the surface, behind each person's mask, may dwell great pain: *breathe . . . might you allow yourself now to just stay with what you are experiencing, just notice . . . What are you aware of now? What is alive for you . . . in you . . . right now . . . breathe into it . . . move if you need to . . . what do you need to feel safe now?*

The right to say 'yes', 'no', and 'STOP!'

We need to have a sense of being able to say 'yes' or 'no', and to understand our limits. Am I able to say 'STOP!' if I do not like what is happening to me, or if I feel unable to tolerate what another person is doing or saying? Am I able to stop myself? When a person has been violated, when choice has been disallowed or punished, a person may be in agony, but unable to respond in a safe way.

They may feel distressed by what they themselves are doing but are unable to stop it, or act or respond in a more beneficial way. Some survivors speak as if they have been taken over or silenced by a part of themselves that is overpowering. One survivor said, 'I feel as if abusive family members are standing right behind me, pulling me back. Words get stuck in my throat. I cannot speak. I cannot move.'

In preparing for our creative journey together, we practise different ways of asserting our right to say 'yes', 'no', and 'stop' (Meekums 2000). For some survivors, even attempting to assert themselves within this neutral context is a struggle. Being encouraged to make a personal choice may be challenging for survivors, who often find freedom for personal expression an alien concept.

In the centre of the room we lay out a large rainbow-coloured parachute with handles around the circumference. We gather around the parachute and, to a background of music, together we rhythmically lift and lower the parachute. The energy generated within the group surprises. The collective actions of the group, lifting and lowering the colourful cloth in harmony, generates an exhilarating, yet soothing, breeze. In addition, the parachute provides a curtain as we extend an invitation to participants to chant in rhythmic call and response as all arms rise together in motion, lifting upwards:

> *I have a right to . . .*
> *I need . . .*
> *I choose . . .*
> *I say No to . . .*
> *I say Yes to . . .*

As the programme develops, and the group bonds and participants grow in confidence, we repeat this energizing activity as a warm-up, or as a lead-in to the session ending. As the colourful rainbow cloak is lifted high above them, participants take it in turns to run underneath the parachute and proclaim a personal intention going forwards.

'You choose your way'

Each session makes time for participants to express symbolically, to listen, to witness, to visualize, remember, imagine, move, and reflect. There are opportunities to explore hopes, fears, and dreams through sharing favourite stories, poems, paintings, photographs, and other artefacts that evoke something of importance from past, present or future. Other activities that participants discover as creatively healing include knitting, felting, cooking, growing plants, pressing flowers, scrapbooking, mask making, face painting, and bubble blowing. Each person is invited to discover her own routes of self-expression and, if she chooses to, to find ways of sharing these with the others.

We repeat invitations to 'choose *your* way'. When a child has been disconfirmed in her identity, and fears reprisals for non-conforming self-expression, she may struggle with choices. Uncertainty is uncomfortable. She hears invitations as instruction, with an anxious concern to 'do it properly', 'get it right'. Our invitation is not about directing participants towards pre-determined, 'ideals' or outcomes. Responding or *not responding* to our invitations may mean acknowledging what cannot be changed, recognizing current anguish or struggling with repeat destructive behaviours. This can be an immense challenge for survivors who perpetually feel dominated by punitive persecutory 'protectors'.

We also offer opportunities: 'I'd like to invite you now to allow the song/poem/story to pass through your awareness. Just notice what you are aware of. No effort. What do you notice? What did you hear? What thoughts, feelings or sensations are evoked in you? What do you imagine? What do you make of what you heard?' But the focus is always on individual choice and response within the group, however this might be understood by an individual and between group members.

When a child endures the unspeakable, their narrative of what was done to them often remains silenced. Memories may be locked inside, blocked or lost to body and soul, but the effects live on, in dreams as nightmares, in sudden, unbidden flashes of terror, panic and recurring despair that seem to make no sense. Sometimes, the prospect of a retelling is so terrifying that the untold story is locked away, frozen in time, or even forgotten:

> *Why can't I remember? Did I make it up? Did the abuse actually happen?*
>
> *I can't tell because he told me something awful will happen.*
>
> *I feel the fear of my mother still rotting inside me.*
>
> *Who will believe me when I cannot remember exactly what went on?*
>
> *I feel such agony in my body. It is like a great darkness in my head. There are dead children buried there.*

One participant, Sheila, found that the process of making poetry freed her from feeling so troubled by the fragments of memories that would suddenly erupt:

> *Tick tock*
> *Locked in a box*
> *No pink frock*
> *only my socks.*
> *The ticking clock*
> *Blocks locks*
> *Tick tock*
> *Locked in a box*
> *The shadow outside*
> *The opening door.*

A flash, a smell, the creaking floor
The crack in the ceiling
I have no feeling
Tick tock
Locked in a box.

We do not encourage direct disclosure of explicit content, as it might trigger undue distress in participants. Instead, we invite oblique sharing of experience across all dimensions of expression. We travel via indirect pathways and cross metaphorical bridges. The intention is to facilitate a safe enough, boundaried distance from anything that might overwhelm, which is protective yet permeable. Participants report a growing openness to fresh possibilities for curiosity, awareness, and acceptance of being, of what is, with themselves and others in the present moment.

We invite transition into the world of *'as if . . .'* – an essential ingredient of dissociation, of journey, play, of metaphor, symbolic, embodied and disembodied experience. We invite participants to embark on a metaphorical, an individual (yet shared) journey. Indeed, the whole programme comprises an individual and shared epic journey.

Week by week, we encourage different forms of expression through the body, allowing what might be hidden to be expressed outwardly through movement, gesture or pose, which may be accompanied by vocalization. We invite the body to speak, encouraging a release of tension, an easing of neuromuscular locks and blocks. At first, participants are understandably tentative about expressing themselves spontaneously in this way. Expression may be minimal at times and shifts may be tiny. All expressions are welcomed as valid contributions to the therapeutic process. As in our circle activities, all offerings are witnessed and mirrored. This respectful repetition of each person's movements, however large or small, validates everything expressed. Insights may be gained as a person becomes aware of where feelings are buried or frozen within. We repeat this group dance every week as a shared healing ritual. As participants grow in confidence and insights, they make shifts in their movements and vocal contributions, which continue to be accepted and mirrored by the group.

Invitations

Play

Winnicott highlighted the playful value of psychotherapy: 'Psychotherapy has to do with two people playing together... where playing is not possible then the work of the therapist is directed toward bringing the patient from a state of not being able to play into a state of being able to play' (1971: 38). Within the containing, transitional space, I model when appropriate authentic, playful, sometimes messy spontaneity. Here is a place where we do not have to 'get it right' – whatever 'right' is. This may be unsettling at first for some participants, who may be familiar with therapists as empathic but aloof. If my aim is to facilitate creativity and safe risk taking, I must be prepared to drop the protection of 'professional' masking in the service of creative risk as transformative. Our hope is that as participants feel safer, they may become confident enough to be willing to risk *playing* in the presence of others. An ability to play rests not only in feeling secure *enough*, but also being able to step into the unknown, to feel free enough to take a risk of being vulnerable, spontaneous, messy, and moreover to allow oneself to experience being with others.

The emphasis is always on each person's and the group's *process* rather than the product, results or evidence of change. Artwork or artefacts are valued for what is evoked in the process of their creation, what they express, what comes alive in the witnessing. We do not create products or performance for admiration or interpretation by others. With this in mind, we emphasize that no prior arts experience is necessary.

Singing, sound, and silence

Singing is rooted in the body, in the expansion of breath and in rhythm. The resonance of sounds, particularly when singing with others in unison or in harmony, has the potential to open up the whole being. When we sing, the space we fill expands as we attune to possibilities, shift sensations, enhance connections. Singing offers opportunities to let go of restrictions and self-consciousness – just for now. Throughout the programme, participants are invited to bring and share songs, poems, and music that help them to feel safe, or inspire them, or evoke a sense of feeling good. A love song addressed to 'a beloved' might be a powerful message from a wise loving self within to an exiled or vulnerable part of the self that needs nurture and comfort. For some participants, it is a revelation that meanings in songs and poems may be multi-layered, multi-faceted, and exquisitely personal.

Participants may at first be reluctant to sing or to allow their voice to be expressed and heard in the group – in the session, participants are allowed to be loud. They can choose from a selection of percussion instruments. We sit in the circle facing outwards, away from the centre of the circle, with eyes closed or open. We invite participants to begin to make sounds, to sing, to experiment with different sounds, rhythms, pitch, volumes, moods. I and the co-facilitator lead, gently at first, warming up with gentle humming and rhythmic accompaniment from opposite sides of the circle. Gradually we generate a soundscape of improvisation, vocalizing free-flowing sounds, rhythmic sounds, singing fragments of recognizable songs, shouting phrases, laughing recklessly, moaning without inhibition, shrieking or wailing. It is an opportunity to relinquish restrictive inhibitions. Sounds are echoed, rhythms mirrored, as instruments are banged and shaken. Gradually participants express themselves more boldly. The soundscape spontaneously rises and falls, morphing in mood, pitch, pace, and intensity between atonal, discordant cacophony and rhythmic, tuneful harmony. With a growing crescendo, the tremendous energy of resonant sound peaks. Liberated from silence and vocal self-consciousness, it seems as if the soundscape might never end. Gradually the wave of sound begins to dissolve as it subsides into silence. There is an almost quivering, unified stillness.

Having allowed the stillness and the sounds of silence to resonate, I gently and quietly begin to sing the chorus of *'This little light of mine, I'm gonna let it shine'*. Group members join in, and the sharing of this well-known song provides a grounding, a return, an intention going forward. The song fades out and we return to silence.

As we reflect on this experience of soundscaping within the group, some participants share an exhilarating sense of liberation at feeling safe enough to give voice, to wail, to shout, sheltered by the chorus of improvized voices and instruments rising and falling. Others do not feel so able to express themselves vocally, yet feel held within the group and 'uplifted' by the freedom being expressed vocally by the other participants. One expressed a wistful sadness as she had felt locked in silence and inner tension, unable to open her throat to allow any vocal expression. There is no right or wrong way to experience any of these activities.

Mask making

Each of us has different aspects and qualities, different faces, different masks that we show to the world, while concealing other parts (Figure 5.3). In creative therapies, there are possibilities for safely revealing previously hidden

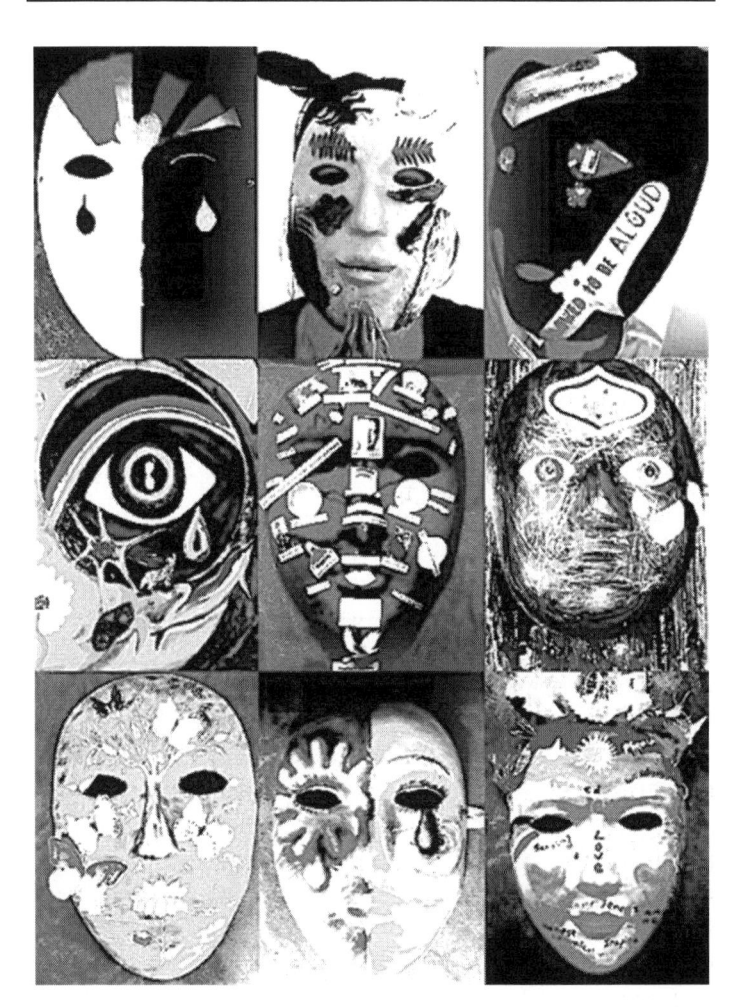

Figure 5.3 Masks

aspects. Mask making offers the opportunity to play with concealing and revealing (Anderson-Warren and Grainger 2000). We might ask participants to ask themselves: 'Who am I? What are the masks I wear and who am I behind my mask/s? With what part or parts of me would I like a better relationship?'

Historically, masks in different cultures have been used in healing, as life-enhancing means for transformation and celebration, and within religious and sacred rituals. Creative mask work potentially holds immense power, which needs to be recognized and respected. It is also vital to understand that masks are also used for malevolent purposes. Abusers, particularly ritualistic and mind control abusers, use masks to deceive, terrify, and subdue their victims. Therapists need to be confident that they can remain alert to the fluctuating needs of individual members within the group, and the group process as the mask work unfolds. The priority is to maintain the safe container that enables creative work with selves that may present themselves through this activity. It is wise to be ready for the unexpected, and always to allow sufficient space and time. When working with survivors of childhood abuse, careful consideration needs to be given to whether mask work is appropriate.

There are many ways of incorporating mask making. For mask work to unfold safely, therapists need to be alert to risks and contraindications, and confident that all parts of a person feel safe enough to participate. With a therapeutic intention, the *both-and* qualities of masks offer space for possibilities to emerge beyond the limitations of existing frames of *either-or*. Mask work processes facilitate transitions from rigid, or polarized, experiencing to an acceptance or acknowledgement of the presence and interaction of contradictory ways of being, acting or thinking. Rejected or neglected aspects of the self may more safely be expressed through symbolic means rather than literal expression. It is another '*as if . . .*' experience.

The creation of a respectful focus in mask work can facilitate an individual's ability to play in ways that allow and invite freer expression. My invitation to play extends an indirect welcome to child parts and younger selves, who may be listening and waiting, and may not yet feel safe enough to emerge. These parts may long for opportunities to feel safe enough to play, perhaps for the first time in their lives. Masks offer participants opportunities to externalize parts of themselves symbolically. This might include aspects of the participant that may not yet have been explicitly articulated or expressed. A mask may offer a tangible container for a person to hold and even express feelings, yearnings, and sensations. For people who have relied on dissociative processes as creative means of survival, mask work validates living with many selves. Participants may become willing to allow younger and/or child selves to emerge and join in the play.

As the shared play develops, participants are invited to disclose, express, and, if appropriate, to let go of protective 'masks' or disguises – at least temporarily – so that in time they might need them less. The aim is validation, compassion, and acceptance of self and others, a better understanding of our different selves. One participant, Daisy, reflected:

> *I found the making of masks gave me a way of telling my story and explaining to others how my mind developed. It allowed me to explain how my mind worked as opposed to being labelled DID; and put into box called DID with people assuming my mind works like everyone else in the box called DID, which has been really upsetting and so very frustrating. Have never liked the term Disorder attached to the end of Dissociative Identity, as to me it is a very logical and ordered way of thinking and responding to trauma and these masks have clarified that to me. Through the masks, parts of my story that I thought I would never ever tell anyone outside of therapy, I have been able to tell in a safe way. My partner now knows about my childhood through these masks, as I could not tell him anything before. I still feel that he must now be looking at me and thinking what a very odd person I am, but he doesn't! I am so surprised!*

Challenges to creative group work

On occasion, the question arises of what we might need to do or what action to take if someone does not keep the group agreement. Ideally, it is group members who should address such difficulties, but this is unlikely with this type of client. The facilitators need to ascertain what, if anything, needs to be said or done to protect the group's boundaries, and the tenets of the group agreement, with the safety of all members the priority.

Some individuals who were sexually abused express a feeling of an uncomfortable gap between themselves and survivors of other forms of childhood abuse. They express a belief that sexual abuse is much worse than other forms of abuse, that sexual violation is far more damaging than beatings or neglect, even when the beatings were constant, severe or ritualized. This can create a division of 'us and them', sometimes unspoken, which creates a challenge for group bonding. One participant reflected that she felt unable to disclose her experience of sexual abuse in the group, as she did not want to 'inflict her descriptions of abuse' on those who might become vicariously traumatized. Correspondingly, survivors of other forms of abuse may feel 'less than', that their experiences of abuse were trivial and that they do not have the right to be part of the group.

To minimize this challenge, we encourage metaphorical, symbolic, abstract personal expression. In the session activities, however, we encourage a focus on the expression of personal experience through oblique and indirect yet meaningful means. We aim to welcome differences while minimizing judgement of potentially divisive and damaging narratives. This does not eliminate the difficulties that can arise through personal disclosures outside group sessions.

The emphasis is on patterns of experience that connect rather than distance. However, the possibility of polarization, splitting, gaps, and ruptures may arise, and needs to be faced. Challenges to group relationships and process include:

- Destructive enactments/transference (e.g. one member dominates, bullies, criticizes others)
- Flashbacks triggered during a session
- Extreme outbursts of fear or rage
- Rigid, polarized beliefs that limit or criticize a person's offering or creations
- Extreme dissociating phenomena
- Non-attendance
- External interactions between group members that have an impact on the group
- External challenges – e.g. a fire alarm, which necessitates evacuation from the venue.

We cannot know what might trigger distress or a flashback. I always ask at the initial assessment meeting if there is anything the person is aware of that might make them feel uncomfortable, such as masks, puppets, music or certain activities. We emphasize that if anything occurs that any participant finds upsetting or triggers distress or concern, our priority is to ensure safety. We may support that person through the activity, or away from the group activity, or change the activity. Each participant is more important than the activity itself. If an individual feels too unsafe or upset to remain in the room, one co-facilitator can attend to that person while the other stays with the group. If someone has become upset or distressed, time is allowed for group members to explore what may have happened, either at that moment or later.

I have been asked how safe it is to use creative visualization, storytelling, drama or movement with dissociating clients as a therapeutic intervention in a group. Might potentially psychotic, dissociating participants 'spiral out of control in some way'? In my experience, this has not been the case. I remain attentive to the shifting self states of group members and alert for the unexpected.

Feedback from participants

All participants are asked to provide feedback during and after the programme. In our young people's programme, 17-year-old Kerry shared in a closing group check-in:

> *It's like we've all got this thing. We've all had a weird thing that's happened to us. Everyone out there thinks we're weird, but in here we're not even though we've all got a different weird thing. So I don't feel so lonely weird now. This creative group work has shown me ways to express my pain and take back control into my life. It has been life changing.*

Brenda reflected:

> *My hopes and expectations of the group were for a place to explore my pain through art, not necessarily to talk or to share, but to work my way through the curve balls life has shown me. I feel I have started to do this through the invitations of Zoë, as I had to think and put into pictures my experiences not just words. Giving voice to the abstract words like sadness, pain, hurt, anger in a group was quite a powerful experience, but I didn't feel as engaged as I wanted to be in the group ... Even so, it has rekindled the creative process and acknowledged the playful inner child who doesn't have to sit around in the dark stuck in pain and sadness. Part of my issue is 'self-isolation' and I was determined to see this experience through to the end, even though I felt like quitting many times. It was almost a test for me to be part of a group where no one really knew me and experiencing their reaction to me is something I would like to explore more.*

And Gill said:

> *I have managed to go out and re-join the gym; I am considering an amateur dramatic group. I am more accepting of my decision to break out of the toxic, co-dependent relationship I had with my family. I may have been to hell and back, but there is beauty in the dark, there is strength in the dark corners. Even a butterfly had to survive in a cocoon before it grew wings and flittered in and out of the shadow. I hold my head even higher knowing that I am in control of my destiny and don't have to surrender to the fate of what happened in my childhood.*

Conclusion

We make meaning through creating, telling, and retelling stories and fragments of stories of our lives. Humans in all cultures have made sense of the rhythms of life through stories, myths, narratives, images, music, movement, and dance. We harness breath, rhythm, tone, pace, pitch, and silence. Our creativity moves us, taps into our emotions. We make associations as we engage with expressive arts forms. As embodied beings, we are always in different kinds of relationship with ourselves and with others, and in our imagination we try to relate beyond our limitations.

Expressive arts in therapy involve risk, a leap into an unknown void of possibility that may change us in the process. It is a messy, unpredictable, and at times chaotic process but, at the same time, vibrant and alive. The arts are an invitation to accept oneself as a whole, wondrous human being, leading into uncharted territory from which there may be no turning back. Where our intention as facilitators bears fruit, participants experience more balanced, beneficial relating between themselves and others. Nurtured within the containing therapeutic circle, where every part of them is welcome, movement towards their own acceptance develops. As survivors move from hurting to healing, they become more able to let go of the suffering of the past, as they live free in today and create better tomorrows.

6

Survivors' experience of the judicial process

Zoë Pool and Ellie Maguire

> Perspectives on reporting abuse to the police • police and court procedures • Victim and Witness Support • the experience of clients who have reported abuse

Hurting to Healing neither encourages nor discourages survivors from reporting to the police. Survivors often have little or no understanding of the criminal justice system, so are unprepared for the challenges they will face if they do report to the police. This chapter provides information about the process, to empower survivors to make choices based on realistic expectations. It aims to increase the knowledge of professionals and others who support survivors through the criminal justice system. Our clients, whose personal narratives are included here, have consented to anonymous inclusion of their experiences.

Since the revelations of Jimmy Savile's systematic abuse of children, there has been a dramatic increase in the number of victims of childhood abuse (particularly sexual abuse) who have reported their abuser(s) to the police. Hurting to Healing clients who have reported say they now feel more confident that they will be believed, and that their case will be investigated seriously. Approximately 20% of our clients have reported their abuser(s) and this number is rising.

Keir Starmer, former Director of Public Prosecutions, has acknowledged that victims of sexual assault have lacked confidence to report offences against them to the police. In historic cases there can be little supporting evidence and often no forensic evidence available. Starmer indicates that the number of victims at risk is likely to be much higher than previously thought, with many vulnerable victims unprotected by the law and at continued risk of abuse. He identifies flaws in the way the credibility and reliability of sexual abuse victims is assessed, and asserts the need for a radical shift in how the police and Crown Prosecution Service address cases of sexual assault against children:

> *If the credibility and reliability of the victims of exploitation in Rochdale were tested solely by asking questions such as whether they reported their abuse swiftly, whether they returned to the perpetrators, whether they had ever told untruths in the past, and whether their accounts were unaffected by drink or drugs, the answers would almost always result in a decision not to prosecute.*
>
> (Starmer 2013)

The police response is changing, leading to re-examination of historic cases that were not adequately investigated, or were left unprosecuted due to lack of evidence.

A survivor's experience of reporting abuse

Edith's confidence to report her abuse developed from her experience of therapy with Hurting to Healing.

> *Through the benefit of therapy with Hurting to Healing, I had understood the complex issues surrounding my own abuse: the manipulation and lies, the power he used in grooming me, and grooming my family, and the threats he made to a young person too vulnerable to understand what was going on. I was brought up in a world where adults were to be respected, you didn't answer back and if you were upset you were 'just being silly'. Thanks to Hurting to Healing, I viewed my abuse from a completely different perspective. I stood outside the circle and looked on as an observer might do. Having raised two children also helped me understand the vulnerability of a child and the simplicity of their understanding and trust. When my children reached the age that I was when the abuse took place, it was plain that I had stood no chance of standing up to him. Through therapy, one of the most powerful things I learnt was that it wasn't my secret – it was his secret. Who had the most to lose should his crimes be revealed? Well, it certainly wasn't me!*

Edith reflected on a documentary about Savile and its impact on her:

> *Like everyone, I was deeply upset and very angry that such appalling abuse had been carried out under everyone's noses: abuse against children and in some cases very ill children and other vulnerable adults. There were many that were complicit, who hadn't wanted to rock the boat in case their careers were damaged. Their careers were more important than the*

safety of children. It was astounding to hear people on television tell us that many knew what was going on and worse. People knew, but they were too cowardly to speak out. The whistle-blower is often shot down in flames and is afforded no protection. We have all witnessed the influence of this documentary. The media began to explore the issues regarding child abuse and ask questions (although not always the right ones). However, it didn't take long before some started to attack Savile's victims, and $\frac{1}{2}$ attempted to minimize what had happened and to trivialize the effects.

As someone who has always felt powerless in this world, someone who has always felt 'afraid' but never been able to pinpoint why, it was empowering to hear others speaking out about their abuse. I am sure I am not alone in feeling the way I did. Whenever I hear about someone else's abuse, it sparks something deep within me: a ferocious anger, frustration with society, great sadness and a feeling of hopelessness.

I could not contain the anger I felt, seeing and hearing people attacking victims of abuse, the interviewer unprepared to interrupt, not interested in the truth. My overriding emotion was anger; I just could not contain it any longer. It was a point of no return. I either went ahead and reported to the authorities or became defined by the fear and self-loathing I felt for myself. The thought of gaining some control was appealing and I obviously took great comfort from an expectation that I would have anonymity. Maybe I was naive, but although more than thirty years had elapsed since my abuse as a child, I also believed that the authorities would investigate. I had felt the beginnings of a 'sea change' in attitudes, despite those that tried to counter it. I had evidence of his involvement in my life and I had told friends, and of course, Hurting to Healing.

Edith decided to go to the police.

I still felt too afraid to telephone the police or to roll up at a police station so I decided to email NSPCC anonymously. They responded by assuring me that I was safe. They encouraged me to disclose the perpetrator's name and I typed his name, sweating profusely, my finger hovering over the 'send' button, eventually finding the courage to click. Immediately, I felt empowered – it's a cliché but so true!!!! The next day I asked a friend to contact the police and that weekend I attended an appointment that had been arranged at Bournemouth Police Station, where I was treated with respect and understanding.

My initial interview was taped and filmed. It lasted three hours. However, I was given regular breaks, could stop whenever I felt it was too difficult, and it was okay to get upset. Everything was explained; it was okay to say when I couldn't remember things. I wasn't expected to remember everything. Further interviews followed as I had forgotten to mention details in the initial interview. I also had documentary evidence to pass on to them, which needed clarification.

Many hours were spent over the next couple of months answering questions, while they made further enquiries. It was a difficult time. Two months later my perpetrator was arrested and I was relieved to find that someone else had reported him as well. The police were very thorough, but I had to lay myself bare for them to investigate. My counselling notes were provided, medical records were given. But naively I was shocked that I had to provide Internet passwords. I found this the most difficult part. He was charged some five months later with several accounts of indecent assault under the 1956 Sexual Offences Act. He insisted he was innocent throughout.

Our clients often say that their motivation to make a police report rests in the hope that their abuser will admit their actions, give an explanation and apologize. This is rare. Some hope that reporting what was done to them will prevent their abuser from further abusing vulnerable young people.

The police investigation

The Code of Practice for Victims of Crime, published in October 2013 and updated in 2015 (Ministry of Justice 2015), sets out a victim's entitlements after reporting a crime to the police, and the obligations to the victim on the part of all criminal justice agencies, including the police, Crown Prosecution Service (CPS), Witness Care Units, and HM Courts and Tribunal Service (HMCTS).

In Dorset and most counties, the police have a Child Abuse Investigation Team. Victims of sexual offences may also contact their local independent Sexual Assault Referral Centre (SARC), which provides confidential advice and support to victims of sexual offences, both recent and historic, whether or not they want to report to the police. If a victim wishes to report, the SARC will support them, and their police interview will often take place in the SARC rather than in the police station. Interview rooms are designed to be as comfortable and relaxed as possible, with discreet cameras in the corner of the room.

After the victim has given their initial statement, the case will be investigated under the direction of the designated Officer in Charge (OIC). Another victim, Pete, described this process:

> *I never expected that the investigation would take so long, and that I would be kept so much in the dark about what was happening. During the investigation, the police gave me very little information. They said*

> it was due to legal restrictions, but I felt ignored and very powerless, like a child again. And because of the silence and feeling blanked, I found it hard to trust that the police were taking me seriously.

Investigations of historic cases usually involve the collection of third-party material. This includes medical records and childhood records such as those retained by schools, social services, children's homes, etc., including notes made by counsellors during therapy. Another victim said:

> I hadn't realized that because I was having therapy, the police could insist that my therapist's notes had to be given over. I refused to give permission but they slapped a court order for the notes to be handed over anyway. It worried me what she had been writing. My therapist told me she felt legally obliged to comply with this or else face a court summons.

And Pete recalled:

> I didn't know what to expect when I signed the consent form for the police. But I didn't expect things I'd told my counsellor about things that had happened to me in my life that had nothing to do with the abuse would be read out. I felt so powerless; and the officer had told me they would edit it to protect me, but they didn't. I felt like I was on trial, I was being 'investigated'. Things I'd done and decisions I'd made and told my counsellor were being scrutinized, were challenged and used against me. I felt violated all over again, with nothing I could do to prevent it.

The role of the CPS

On completion of the investigation, unless there has been an admission of guilt by the alleged abuser, the police hand the case to the Crown Prosecution Service, who decide whether or not to prosecute, based on whether there is enough evidence to support a prosecution, and whether it is in the public interest to do so. This is called the Full Code Test.

A decision not to prosecute has a profound impact on victims, who are denied the possibility of seeking justice for crimes committed against them. Pete reflected:

> *I was gutted when they told me they were dropping it because there was not enough evidence. I felt no one believed me. Everyone would think I'd made it all up. It all ended so suddenly, no justice, and I just felt humiliated.*

The Victims' Right to Review Scheme makes it possible for a victim to appeal a CPS decision not to prosecute, where the decision has been made on or after 5 June 2013. More information can be found on the CPS website.

If the CPS decides to prosecute, it will go to trial unless the accused pleads guilty. Investigations of childhood abuse often take a year or more to gather evidence. During this time victims can feel like their life is 'on hold'. Third-party materials are disclosed to the defence team, who share them with the accused, enabling the accused to instruct their legal representative. Their views must be represented at trial, as they have the right to defend themselves. However, the victim is often not prepared for this disclosure, so support from therapists, friends, and family is vital throughout the process.

The trial

Cases of childhood abuse are tried at a Crown Court. After a long wait for the trial date to be confirmed, victims (the complainants) are usually called as witnesses for the prosecution. Sam struggled with the delay. He recalled:

> *I felt invaded all over again, realizing that the perpetrator and his defence team had access to my childhood records or notes my counsellor made. When I was called to give evidence in the court, it was terrifying, even though I had been on a court visit and Victim Support had showed me around and told me what to expect. I thought I had been doing so well, and had been feeling much better, but waiting and waiting for the trial and fearing what would happen, and seeing him being there, all my flashbacks got worse. The police wanted to show me my video evidence and that was awful. Hearing myself describe it all and all the details, it felt like torture, like me back there as a child being abused all over again.*

Increasing anxiety about the court process puts considerable stress on victims. Edith recalled:

> *I was asked if I wanted any 'special measures' in court and requested a screen to shield me. I didn't want to see him, and I didn't want him to see me! I honestly couldn't have coped without that screen. Couldn't bear to see his face again while having to recount what he did to me. I would have contacted Hurting to Healing more often during the investigation – the police made it clear that I was at liberty to do so; in fact, they encouraged it if it would help. I got the impression this was a 'new thing' – that previously such support would have been frowned upon. However, I also knew that any further sessions would have to be divulged by way of evidence; anything pertinent would then be disclosed to the defence. This made me reluctant to seek further support, as it was another thing I would be forced to reveal.*
>
> *I remember calling my counsellor at Hurting to Healing shortly before the trial and breaking down. There was a backlash in the press because some high-profile*

offenders had been found 'not guilty'. Their accusers were being labelled as false accusers and there were statements made that they should be 'outed'. No one explained the burden of proof. No one explained the definition of a 'not guilty' verdict. There were also calls for anonymity to be provided to those accused, something not given to people who were accused of murder.

At this point, I contacted the police and said I was having second thoughts. *I felt the stress was too much and I was beginning to feel unwell as a result. They assured me that I would have a screen while giving evidence and they again convinced me that the case against him was a strong one.*

One policewoman told me that in her experience of child abuse cases, an 'expert witness' in the form of a psychiatrist is often required to convince the jury of the damage done and by implication the guilt of the accused. Sadly, the cost of such a witness normally equates to about £5,000, which means that it is rarely sanctioned. Many abusers get off because of this lack of expertise. How can this be justice?

Witnesses classified as vulnerable or intimidated witnesses (VIWs – sections 16 and 17 of the Youth Justice and Criminal Evidence Act 1999) can choose to apply for special measures at court, designed to help make it easier for them to give evidence. Potential VIWs should be identified in advance of trial so that an application for special measures can be made by the officer in charge of the case. The presiding judge decides whether to grant special measures. These include giving evidence behind a screen, or via a live link (in another room, connected live to the courtroom), or an intermediary for those who have difficulty communicating, such as speech impairment or learning disability.

Interviews recorded by the police, rather than written, can be used as a victim's 'evidence in chief' at trial. DVD interviews can be played to the jury, so the victim does not have verbally to describe their experiences again in court. The defence may then cross-examine the victim.

The Witness Service

The Witness Service, run by Citizens' Advice, is present at crown and magistrates' courts across England and Wales, providing support and information before and during trial. The volunteers are carefully selected, trained, and supervised by paid staff. The Service offers a visit to the court before the day of trial, including a tour of the courtroom and waiting facilities, explanations of court procedures, and a demonstration of special measures such as a live link. The Service cannot advise witnesses what questions they will be asked or rehearse evidence in any way. This is called 'coaching'. One victim reported:

> *I found it really helpful to see the courtroom for myself. I was shown around and told who would be where and what to expect. It was all very different from what I'd seen on TV. I hadn't realized that anyone could go to hear the trial in the public gallery. I was told about procedures, about when I could talk to friends who were also witnesses in the same case. It had been a shock to me when someone told me that it was no longer 'my case' – it was 'The Crown's case against . . .'. I became just another witness. That felt very odd. They were keen for me to see my interview again, and to read my first statement, they said – to refresh my memory – as if I could forget!*

The Witness Charter describes what witnesses can expect at court and what the courts should provide for witnesses, including a separate waiting area for prosecution and defence witnesses, an alternative entrance to the building for VIWs, and an opportunity to meet the prosecuting barrister before giving evidence. Victims and witnesses are met and supported by the Witness Service volunteers. Witnesses who have made a written statement have an opportunity to read it in the waiting area. Where DVD recordings of a police interview are being used as 'evidence in chief', an opportunity to view the interview is provided before the trial, so the victim can refresh his or her memory.

Here are Edith's reflections on different aspects of this pre-trial period:

Although the trial was due to take place in London, the police urged me to visit Bournemouth Court to see a court room and to be able to sit in the witness box with a screen and see how that felt. I had not intended to visit, as I was concerned that it would frighten me more. However, I went and many of my fears were reduced.

Apart from that visit and the odd phone call from police, there was no other support. I had been given a witness service telephone number, but didn't feel comfortable making the call. I felt I shouldn't be asking for information, but I desperately wanted to feel 'part of what was going on'. I found the Victims Code online and when I did phone Witness Support at the court, I expected some information regarding the process, but was just asked what I wanted to know. I didn't know where to start! I was merely told about the logistics of arriving on the day. Facing the court process as a witness is very daunting and the lack of information only elevates the stress. I received no advice or preparation by the CPS/police before the trial.

I also don't understand why I wasn't told about his defence. His defence was revealed on day one of the case. Why couldn't I be told this? I knew nothing of his defence. No one told me, despite it being disclosed on the first day of the trial, that he was denying having ever known me. Why is so little information about the trial process given to the victim? I had tried to prepare myself emotionally and practically for the trial. I thought about what they would ask me, I thought about the right words to use . . . so difficult to explain the complexity of emotions. And it was painful to have to re-visit the abuse and experience again that horrible, horrible time. Only those who've walked in your shoes truly understand what it's like.

It was particularly difficult to tell my children about the abuse and the imminent trial. They were shocked and I knew they were trying to keep their emotions in check, even though on the outside mine were contained. It was difficult to keep working, mothering, the date coming nearer and nearer, worrying about them, the effect on them, feeling selfish because I may have jeopardized their security.

Apart from having to divulge to my children, by far the worse part of the whole thing was the press intrusion. Unfortunately, as my perpetrator was someone of notoriety, the press were keen to cover the story. His notoriety was why I had not reported him and I was afraid of the power of the media. As soon as he was arrested, the press gave him a platform to deny his crimes and gain public sympathy, further intimidating his victims and those that would have to go through a public trial. I began to fear for my own safety and that of my family and my witnesses. My witnesses also felt intimidated. Public denials only served to prejudice a forthcoming jury and further intimidate victims. Furthermore, during the trial everyone (including friends, my children and husband) was able to read explicit details of my abuse.

I feared this might discourage many victims from reporting to the police and I was unprepared for this explicit coverage.

Giving evidence

Many victims who give evidence at trial find the experience extremely distressing, especially when they hear the accused's defence for the first time. This may involve total denial of the victim's allegations, which can overwhelm the victim, or the dispute of particular facts. It is difficult to prepare for this experience. Defence barristers have a duty to provide a robust defence for their client and may infer that the victim is untruthful, inaccurate or unreliable. The victim is expected to respond to assertions and questions put by the defence barrister in cross-examination. This can be extremely difficult given the personal nature of the offences involved and the difficulty of recalling events that took place years before. Victims can feel that the accused is gaining some satisfaction from having seen or heard their emotional reactions. Witnesses can ask the presiding judge for a break to compose themselves, should they become emotional or need a comfort break during evidence. Edith remembered:

While waiting to go into court, one ex-policeman went to great lengths to ensure I didn't run into my perpetrator in the corridor or lift. He sat with me and said, 'This is your chance to tell them what happened, your chance to tell the truth and in doing so expose his lies.' That was powerful. I can honestly say, I have never been so nervous in my life. However, I also felt angry that I had to go through all this because of him. His lack of humility had meant that he had denied all of the offences, strenuously denied any guilt and continued to lie.

I met the prosecuting barrister five minutes before I entered the courtroom. Her advice was basic: 'Just answer the questions, "yes" or "no", don't try to explain, don't try and be clever and second guess where the defence barrister's questions are coming from. If you are upset, try not to cry.' This was daunting but more importantly, I liked her and felt confident that she would try her utmost to expose the truth.

With this advice I entered the courtroom. I answered 'yes' or 'no', but I just knew that the jury were not going to believe me unless I explained. So, I explained. I told them how I felt, how frightened I was, how I didn't understand, how it hurt, how I was afraid as a child to tell the truth, fearing I would lose everything!

One of the greatest fears expressed regarding the court process is being verbally attacked by the defence barrister, and called a liar in public. Edith recalled:

The defence barrister, like an actor on the stage, gave the performance of his life. He laughed at me, appeared angry when accusing me of lying, feigned shock when I told him his client was a liar. He tried to repeat the same question many times but the judge was not having any of it. He tried every angle, even lying about one of my witness's evidence, to get a reaction. He made me angry; he tried to make me cry. It was an Oscar–winning performance, but I knew the truth and I knew my offender was a liar. His privileged upbringing did him no favours and frankly it all turned into a bit of a pantomime performance. 'Oh yes he did, oh no he didn't!' My offender was caught out by his lies and his ever shifting moral compass when recounting 'just how it was back then'. I was in court for two days and each time I left for a break I just felt anger. The judge was supportive, offered me regular breaks and made it clear when he didn't like the line of questioning. In actual fact, although I found the trial difficult and extremely stressful, I didn't find the questioning difficult, because I just told the truth. If I couldn't remember, I said I couldn't remember. It was ridiculous to expect me to be able to remember little details. But he didn't like the fact that I could remember and describe the abuse, the grooming techniques and the threats he had used to prolong the weeks and months of his crimes.

Sam reported:

Before the trial started, and when it got under way, I was surprised how long I was kept waiting. Waiting for the case to be approved for trial, and more waiting before finally being called to give my evidence. This was one of the worst things – how long it all went on. It was as if my whole life was on hold. And the trial was the most important thing in my life and it just dragged on and on. Then on the day, I felt totally exposed, stripped bare – all over again.

Victims often have a strong reaction to members of the public in the public gallery, especially family or friends of the defendant, whom the victim may know. The victim is unable to control this, as criminal cases are open for public viewing, although giving evidence behind a screen usually means that those in the public gallery cannot see the victim when they give evidence. If a victim knows that particular individuals will be sitting in the gallery, this can heighten anxiety and affect their ability to give clear and confident evidence in the witness box. Victims may also be worried about their own friends and family members seeing or sitting near to the defendant's supporters. These are the thoughts of one victim:

It was horribly distressing, giving evidence and being cross-examined, but I felt I'd stood up for me, spoken out about what was done to me. Finally, I no longer needed to hide or feel ashamed, as I'd done nothing wrong. It wasn't my fault. It was very scary though. In that moment he no longer had power over me. But it didn't stop me worrying later that something terrible might happen to me, like he had threatened. All the family were there staring, and I felt their hate, that I was a betrayer.

Depending on the facilities available and the layout of the court building, it is not always possible to prevent the victim seeing those who have come to view the trial on the way to or from the courtroom, during cigarette breaks or during the lunch hour.

Victims may have concerns about press reports. Although journalists do not always report cases of childhood abuse, it is more likely to happen if a defendant is in the public eye, a teacher or priest. Reports may be printed during the trial, at the verdict or at sentencing. While the names of child victims cannot be printed without their permission (even if they are now adults), the defendant's name is usually printed unless they are under 18. One victim recalled:

I was shocked at how much detail was reported in the papers about what the abusers did to me. I live in a small town in Dorset, and everybody knew it was me, even though I was promised that my identity would be concealed. I was told that there would be restrictions on what could be reported, but the amount of detail in the paper made it easy for everyone to work out who the victim was – people started treating me differently, remarks were made. It was really upsetting.

The verdict and beyond

Victims and other witnesses are informed of the outcome of the trial when the jury have reached their verdict. Juries are encouraged to deliberate until all twelve members can agree on a verdict. If this is not possible, they try to reach a majority verdict. This term can be confusing for victims, who may presume that a majority verdict means majority in the literal sense, but a majority verdict at crown court can only be reached when at least ten members of the jury agree on a verdict. If after thorough deliberation the jury are unable to reach a majority verdict – a 'hung jury' – the CPS decides whether to proceed to a re-trial.

When jurors acquit defendants, optimism about justice and a conviction can turn to disillusion, anger, and fear. Complainants feel invalidated, or feel labelled as liars. Such a verdict can cause immediate shock and distress for the victim. One victim described it as follows:

> *I felt my life was over when I heard the not guilty verdict. I choked. I could hardly breathe. I felt flooded with shame – as if no one believed me. I think he got off because there were bits I couldn't remember. Important bits. The defence barrister called me a liar because I couldn't remember everything. I must have sounded . . . as if everybody thought I was lying. I wished I was dead, that I'd never reported him. I wanted to die and I wanted to kill him too. I did not cope at all well. I thought I would never get over the shame. My counselling really helped me to keep going. I was put in touch with other survivors who had been through this.*

Over time, and with the right care and support, some victims feel that the experience was beneficial overall. The police and CPS have believed them, supported their claim and attempted to prosecute, and they were brave enough to report the offence initially and to uphold their account publicly in court. Victims are no longer left wondering 'what if', which can enable them to focus more fully on personal recovery and wellbeing.

Edith recalled:

He was found guilty and it was such a relief. Now the trial is over and my abuser is in prison, I feel like one of the lucky ones. Statistics bear this out! According to the government's own figures, fewer than one in thirty victims can expect to see her or his attacker brought to justice.

I still feel angry, I will never forgive him for what he did, and that anger was compounded by the lies he told throughout the process. I have no regrets, not one single one! It's still hard to believe that it is over and done with. Getting back to normality after a court case takes time. The trial takes over everything. Automatic pilot kicks in, but your head is in a different universe.

I was so glad I attended court on the day of sentencing. Although I was nervous, I felt I had to go. I got the opportunity to thank those I'd met in the police, the barrister who represented me, the witness support staff. I also had the opportunity to meet some of the others who had made complaints, whose crimes had not been part of the indictment but part of the bad character evidence. I was glad to feel 'part of a team' that had hopefully, by virtue of the guilty verdict, empowered others to report crimes against them.

I was very moved by the words of the judge. He made it clear that these offences were not trivial, despite the attempts by the media to minimize. He told everyone that had these crimes been committed today they would have been deemed 'rape' offences and he could have been imprisoned for life as a result. All the victim impact statements were read out, which were harrowing, but they left no one in that courtroom with any doubt that this man was evil and his crimes despicable.

After a guilty verdict, sentencing will often be scheduled several weeks later. This allows time for a pre-sentence report to be written in relation to the perpetrator, and for the victim to write their Victim Personal Statement (VPS), which the judge reads in advance of the hearing. This statement enables victims to express to the court how the crime has affected them, including impact upon relationships, employment, social isolation, and physical and psychological wellbeing. Victims can choose to read their VPS aloud at the sentencing hearing; otherwise, the judge may refer to or quote passages from the VPS before delivering the sentence. Although the VPS cannot dictate what sentence is delivered, the judge considers the impact of the crime upon the victim. Information relating to the offender, including previous convictions and personal circumstances, are also considered.

Many victims need adequate support before and after sentencing because of the emotional impact involved. Sam reflected:

I had expected to feel elated, free even, but experienced a dull, gnawing, anti-climax in the hours, days and weeks following sentencing. Even though he had been brought to justice and punished, I didn't feel any better, or less emotional or afraid. The case had dragged on for so long, it had swallowed up my life, and readjusting, finding a focus for the future was hard. My family and friends expected me to just move on, and the reality that I still felt so low was a bit of a shock really.

After the investigation and trial, family and friends may expect that the victim will finally let go of the past and get on with their lives, especially if the perpetrator is found guilty. Some victims, however, continue to suffer even when the verdict is 'guilty'. They fear reprisals by the abuser or their associates. This can be so even when the offender is behind bars. In cases where the perpetrator is acquitted or the case dismissed, victims report their struggle to cope. Apart from feeling they were not believed, they have endured an ordeal, and once again their abuser has 'got away with it'. Fears of the perpetrator's power to abuse, manipulate or to harm them or their family endure. Concerns that abusers are free to continue abusing young people remain a real threat to peace of mind.

Conclusion

Some victims who have sought justice have been stalked and threatened, exposed to the press, and poorly protected by the police. They may find it hard to overcome fears of being judged by others, that their motives will be judged negatively either for reporting at all or for not reporting sooner. They fear that others' judgements might affect their or their family's future. For some, the many consequences of the crimes committed against them can have far-reaching effects on their ability to live well. Survivors may need continued long-term therapeutic support as they seek to cope and recover from the ongoing impact of their childhood trauma.

Resources for clients and counsellors

The Code of Practice for Victims of Crime:

https://www.gov.uk/government/publications/the-code-of-practice-for-victims-of-crime

Guidelines on Prosecuting Cases of Child Sexual Abuse:

http://www.cps.gov.uk/legal/a_to_c/child_sexual_abuse

The Full Code Test:

https://www.cps.gov.uk/publications/code_for_crown_prosecutors/codetest.html

Starmer, K. (2013) The criminal justice response to child sexual abuse: time for a national consensus, speech, 6 March. Available at:

http://www.cps.gov.uk/news/articles/the_criminal_justice_response_to_child_sexual_abuse_-_time_for_a_national_consensus

Information about VIWs and special measures is available in the Witness Charter:

https://www.gov.uk/government/publications/the-witness-charter-standards-of-care-for-witnesses-in-the-criminal-justice-system

http://www.cps.gov.uk/legal/s_to_u/special_measures

Further information can be found at:

https://www.gov.uk/government/uploads/system/uploads/attachment_data/file/264625/victims-vps-guidance.pdf

7

A practitioner's experience of the judicial process

Gail Longhurst

> The counsellor's notes • supporting clients through the court process • the first police interview • preparing for court • in the witness stand • waiting for the verdict

Increasing acceptance that access to therapeutic services during the court process is beneficial to clients who may be called as witnesses has accompanied the shift in how historical childhood abuse cases are addressed by the law. Correspondingly, more counsellors are now called to give statements to the police, to submit their notes and records to the police or the Crown Prosecution Service (CPS), and to appear in court as witnesses of fact. This change creates an obligation on the part of counsellors to keep notes with a possible judicial process in mind. Court proceedings often involve a client's personal information, which may appear irrelevant to the case, to be disclosed. This leaves counsellors feeling uncertain and cautious about what to write in their notes.

The counsellor's notes

At Hurting to Healing, when the limits of confidentiality are explained to clients during their initial assessment, the possibility that the police or the CPS might require notes is emphasized. Hurting to Healing has created a notes and record-keeping protocol that supports any possible requirements, and is in accordance with the guidelines for data protection. The agency now asks counsellors to submit their notes in a uniform template for regular archiving. This archive is kept in a secure encrypted section of the administrator's hard drive. This means that even if, much later, when the client or perhaps even the counsellor has left the agency, the client requires support from the notes, they are readily available with the client's permission. Based on my own experience, I decided that I would also hold client files indefinitely in my private practice where they related to any form of abuse. There is no way of knowing if or when any client may report to the police. I now want to be sure I have such client notes available regardless of the passing of time. Hurting to Healing counsellors are also encouraged to discuss their note taking and record keeping with their supervisors, to ensure that they comprehend what may be expected of them in the event of a court case.

Writing client notes is very personal, but I was fortunate to have benefited previously from guidance at a police training centre in preparation for working with survivors of domestic violence and honour crimes. Having been referred by the police, some of these clients were in the court process. Notes need to provide a factual account of what the client said, although this need not be verbatim; this includes when the incident(s) happened, where it/they occurred, and who was involved. It is not for the therapist to include interpretations or any form of process notes. This factual style of note writing was to prove helpful when, as I describe below, I appeared as a 'witness of fact'. There was no expectation that I would, or could, give an expert opinion. It is the role of an expert witness to give opinions on the facts of the case. This individual will have a level of experience and qualification that informs opinions given where matters are not within the common knowledge of the court (Bond and Sandhu 2005: 60):

> *A witness of fact is someone who is called to give evidence about what happened in a case. They are asked to recall what they saw or heard during an incident but not to give opinions. There is a requirement to discuss the facts they remember or have recorded in notes.*
>
> (Bond and Sandhu 2005: 57)

The judicial process therefore has an impact on the types of note taking appropriate in counselling practice. Counsellors need to comply with requirements for access to all therapeutic records, both by the prosecution and the defence. It is a serious offence to change or destroy any written records after a legal request or court order.

In order that any legal process is uncontaminated by what happens in counselling, practitioners who work with clients before or during a trial need a grasp of the judicial process and their responsibilities within it. There may be tensions between the client's need for confidentiality and the public interest for disclosure of potential evidence for prosecuting alleged offenders. Counsellors need to avoid leading questions that might unintentionally coach or rehearse the client. Care must also be taken to ensure that interventions and responses do not influence clients lest they unintentionally absorb in their own memories the counsellor's perspectives on what happened. Counsellors also need to abstain from seeking to differentiate fact from fantasy in the client's narrative, as this might contaminate evidence.

It is understandable that counsellors have concerns about how their notes, especially their process notes, might be used in court. Bond and Mitchels write: 'The distinctive feature of process notes is that they contain information about the subjective processes of the therapist.' They go on to comment that: 'these are subjective notes that are being used in a legal culture where objectivity rules, and therefore, are frequently misunderstood' (2008: 68–9). Process notes may include personal reflections from the therapist's own experience that give insight into the client's sense of self and the therapist's sense of self, and their co-created worldview within the therapeutic relationship. However, barristers sometimes use the counsellor's notes as a means of discrediting both the victim's evidence and the counsellor's expertise (Bond and Mitchels 2008: 69). It is clear from the way defence barristers question victims, in a manner known as 'impeachment', in which they challenge and discredit the witness, that their role is not always one of respecting the veracity of witnesses of fact, but sadly it is permissible in law (Bond and Sandhu 2005: 67).

From my experience of appearing as a witness, it is helpful for notes and records to be clear, simple, and factual, and to include dates, times, and names of any persons involved in the perpetration of an alleged crime. If called as a witness, counsellors need to be able to explain anything written in their notes simply and clearly to the court. Bond and Mitchels comment:

Probably the best way of avoiding or minimizing the difficulties posed by process notes is to review one's

> record keeping practices. *Active weeding out of process notes that are not an essential part of the client record and are no longer relevant to the therapeutic process and securely destroying these is a viable option. This destruction must take place before a legal request for disclosure is received.*
>
> (Bond and Mitchels 2008: 70)

Bond and Mitchels also say that if therapists 'could be confident that these notes would be treated respectfully within the legal process, then [keeping process notes] would be much less of an issue' (2008: 70).

Supporting clients through the court process

Having appeared for the first time as a 'witness of fact' for the prosecution, my experience of and learning from supporting a client through the judiciary process provides an insight into being placed in such a position. Apart from the inevitable ethical dilemmas about confidentiality, it is important to consider the practicalities of preparing clients and oneself to appear in court.

When I first heard that my client had reported her abuser to the police, which I had not expected to happen, and was as a consequence considering returning to therapy, I felt a huge sense of responsibility to ensure any evidence I might be called upon to give was robust, and that the therapy in this pre-trial period did not jeopardize a successful outcome. While I am sure my client felt anxious, I too felt under great pressure to get things right. I knew that appropriate supervision, from an experienced supervisor, was key; and my supervisor at Hurting to Healing steered me to a very valuable and informative document, 'The provision of therapy for vulnerable or intimidated adult witnesses prior to a criminal trial – practice guidance' (CPS 2014).

This document states that 'concern had been expressed that witnesses, including vulnerable or intimidated adult witnesses, have been denied therapy pending the outcome of a criminal trial for fear that their evidence could be tainted and the prosecution lost'. It recognizes that 'this fear may conflict with the need to ensure that vulnerable or intimidated adult victims are able to receive, as soon as possible, immediate and effective treatment to assist their recovery' (CPS 2014: 2). However, it is important to bear in mind that 'the key issue with regard to pre-trial discussions of any kind is the potential effect on the reliability, actual or perceived, of the evidence of the witness and the weight which will be given to it in court' (CPS 2014: 5). It is essential for the therapist to keep this potential conflict in mind throughout the therapeutic process.

On a practical level, my client had been assessed and counselled within Hurting to Healing, and I had been supervised by an experienced Hurting to Healing supervisor. Therefore, there was a paper trail within the agency of how this client had consistently presented her narrative, all of which predated her reporting to the police. Both my client and myself were able to call upon the experience and support network of Hurting to Healing through the court process, and I felt really contained in that knowledge. I wonder if therapists in private practice might feel isolated, especially if their supervisor is unable to be readily available to them.

My first police interview

When my client first contacted me, her message contained permission for me to speak with the police and to disclose all that she had shared with me. The police showed me an informed consent duly signed by my client, which also gave her permission for me to release *all* my client notes to the police. However, this posed an ethical dilemma: my records did not only contain information regarding her childhood abuse. We had also explored other issues that concerned my client and, while I had her consent to give the police access to this information, I did not believe it was ethical to do so. The complete notes would potentially give the abuser information about my client and other people that were nothing to do with the historic abuse.

I did not, therefore, believe it was appropriate to hand all this over to the police knowing that it may be shared through the exchange of documents between the prosecution and defence, and then to the alleged abuser. The police assured me that they would speak with the prosecutor about my concerns. However, the reality is that I could not know what would be included, or excluded, until I was waiting to give evidence on the day of the trial.

According to the practice guidance:

> *If, as will usually be the case, a therapist, having taken appropriate legal advice, believes that the material should not be disclosed, he or she may oppose the witness summons application ... Those aspects of therapy that have no material relevance to criminal proceedings should not have to be disclosed. However, the issue of relevance may need to be reviewed at various and at different stages of the criminal case, as more becomes known about the prosecution and defence cases.*
> (CPS 2014: 6).

While I was treated respectfully by the police throughout my interview, I was left in no doubt that, if I did not hand over all my client records, a court order would be requested and probably granted, since my client had already given the police written consent and contacted me directly to also give her consent. On reflection, I wonder if a refusal to provide my records would be interpreted by the court as showing a lack of cooperation, or if my client might feel that I was being unsupportive. However, Bond and Mitchels note that a therapist could request leave to attend a Directions Hearing: where 'there are significant issues of privacy involved for either the client or the therapist, a judge can be asked to review the evidence and decide what is relevant and therefore available for use in the case' (2008: 70).

The ethical dilemma for therapists is that since the issue of relevance is potentially subject to review, a therapist cannot guarantee that confidentiality will be maintained in all circumstances. This needs to be clearly pointed out to the client as soon as we are advised that he or she has reported to the police. There is a question as to whether counsellors should make this issue about confidentiality clear to the client at the beginning of therapy, or when there is the first revelation of abuse of the kind that could lead to a judicial process. The counsellor cannot of course know early on whether or not a client is likely to go to the police – and in any case no counsellor would want to either encourage or discourage such a step. Yet might such a warning about confidentiality prevent a client from speaking freely?

Following my initial statement to the police, I was interviewed again to clarify the content of my statement. The police also interviewed me shortly before the trial commenced in order to provide a statement covering my contact with my client during the pre-trial period. During every interview, I made sure that the officers were aware that my client had requested a return to counselling, and they in turn informed the Crown Prosecution Service. When my client first contacted the police, her weekly therapy sessions had come to an end. Hurting to Healing offered further counselling to support her through the legal process, in accordance with practice guidance (CPS 2014). My client chose to access therapy on very few occasions, but it was important to know that support was in place, appropriate boundaries were set, and for my additional client notes to be made available to the court. During any counselling or contact with my client, I was constantly aware of the impact of the therapy on her and my evidence at the trial. I thought it was important to clarify these limitations from the outset. Our work would focus on reducing her anxiety about going to court in order to help my client's confidence, but we would avoid any further exploration of the historic events, as that might be interpreted as coaching.

Once all my evidence had been given, there was very little contact with the police while evidence was collected from other witnesses. Finally, all the evidence was presented to the CPS, for them to decide whether the case would proceed to trial. It took seventeen months from my first contact with the police for the case to go to court.

Preparing for court

On the day before attending court, the police confirmed that I would be allowed to have my client notes in the courtroom. It was a relief to know that I was not expected to memorize sessions that had taken place some time previously. On the day of the trial, I was given a copy of the client notes that I had submitted as evidence. This was the first time that I knew the CPS had redacted those parts of my notes that were not relevant to the charges brought against the defendant.

I had spent many hours studying my notes, trying to second-guess what questions I might be asked. From my notes I noticed patterns and themes that often occur when working with survivors of childhood abuse. I checked through my terminology, and wondered what might be taken out of context. What about those emotive words that clients sometimes use? In reality, there is no way of knowing what the prosecution or defence barristers will ask, and not knowing is a very uncomfortable place to be.

I found visiting a local court really helpful. While this was not the court where the trial would take place, it did help me to envisage how it might be to appear in court. Seeing the courtroom demystified the legal environment. I found talking with Victim Support helped me with my thoughts about how things would be on the day. They also gave me insight into the care they were offering to my client, which was reassuring given the uncertainty of the eventual verdict.

As the trial date drew closer, it became increasingly difficult to avoid media coverage of it. However, I wanted to ensure that my evidence was based purely on what my client had revealed during our therapy sessions and was not tainted by public speculation, so I tried as hard as I could to avoid reading it.

In the witness stand

In a room in the court building I waited with other prosecution witnesses. This felt quite surreal: to be in a room of strangers, all with a common cause, but none of us able to talk about it. In my mind I speculated that each one of us might have what felt like a different but important piece of the puzzle. I had to make sure I did not divulge anything to them or inadvertently glean something from them. In our modern world it would also be natural to reach for the tablet or mobile phone, yet they carried the danger of 'up to the minute' news headlines that might be about the trial.

There was no way of knowing precisely when I would be called to give evidence, or how long that might take. The schedule seemed very fluid. This uncertainty led me to wonder whether the proceedings might run over to the following day, and the impact that would have on my diary and my other clients. There is no control over when witnesses will be called, and I found this a very difficult situation to be in. For therapists seeing other clients during the time of the trial, it is important to ensure that there are contingency arrangements in place, since there is always the possibility of re-scheduling by the court.

From my previous experience, I knew that courts could feel quite theatrical. I wondered if that was how it would feel for me, and likewise for the jury? I was determined to stride confidently into the courtroom (and it was quite a walk from the door to the witness stand!) and to come across as a woman who is both comfortable and sure of her evidence. As I entered the courtroom, I took the opportunity to orientate myself to my surroundings, in particular the position of the jury.

Having settled, I drew on the skills that every therapist uses when we are with our clients, and that is to try to form a relationship – but in this case with the jury. But here there was no two-way dialogue to help that relationship along; instead, I tried to make eye contact with individual members of the jury whenever possible, and to direct my responses directly to them. As it turned out, the questions posed by counsel for the prosecution and defence were all factual. I could not have planned for their questions other than being fully conversant with my notes. The defence did attempt to take one sentence in my notes out of context, but I knew that it was important to trust that the prosecution would do their job and clarify the point in question for the jury.

Waiting for the verdict

Having given my evidence, there was no more required of me by the court. There was nothing I could do to influence the outcome. I had tried to be objective, and I needed to remain objective, thinking particularly of what the experience of giving evidence might have been like for my client, and wondering how she felt as she too waited for the verdict. Anything I felt would be much greater for her, and monitoring my own feelings would to some extent help when we came to meet again after the trial.

I first heard the news of his conviction on the radio. The word 'guilty' felt so sweet, bringing tears to my eyes. Now the world would see the defendant as the sex offender he was judged to be. I felt so happy for my client that I could have jumped for joy. My client had previously received a telephone call from an officer assigned to her case, and she shared this with me later. The judge had commented that, 'if some of the assaults had occurred today they would be considered rape'. This acknowledgement of the seriousness of the perpetrator's crime was important for my client to hear.

It was some time before we actually met, but on this occasion the usual counsellor and client boundaries were set aside and we hugged.

Conclusion

It had been my privilege to take some small part in supporting my client through to her day in court. There is a fine line between containing a client supportively to face the unknown of the court process and the even greater uncertainty of the verdict, while avoiding any suggestion of rehearsal or coaching that may jeopardize the outcome of the case. I know how important it had been for me to prepare adequately for appearing in court, checking through my notes many times, trying not to anticipate questions that either counsel might ask. I learned the need to shield myself from social media and the news in general, as these might serve to taint my evidence, or even jeopardize the case.

Through this experience I have learned to prepare for a potential court appearance from my first session with any new client. In the process of agreeing a contract and setting boundaries, my clients need to be properly informed that my notes may be required in court in the event that they choose to disclose a crime against them. This enables my clients to make informed choices around what they disclose to me. I regularly review my client notes to ensure they are an accurate representation of my therapeutic work, but will withstand a legal challenge and the inspection of my clients. I safeguard these in the knowledge that, for some, disclosure might be many years in the future.

Most important for me was the strong support around me of a network of appropriately qualified and experienced supervisors and the whole team at Hurting to Healing. I already had a strong sense of hopefulness for each new client to realize something of their potential; but in addition now I have personally had proof that even when a crime was committed decades ago, there is still hope of justice for adults abused in childhood.

8

Supervising practitioners working with abuse

Michael Jacobs

> *Is supervising abuse counselling different? • care of supervisees • the centrality of counter-transference • effects of abuse work on supervisees • necessary areas of knowledge • handling particular presentations • secondary traumatization • group supervision • agency and organizational contexts • notes for legal processes • supervision and consultancy for supervisors*

Having been involved in setting up at least two agencies for counselling survivors of abuse, my late wife, Moira Walker, stressed in her practice and her teaching the need for good supervision. She delivered several (unpublished) lectures and developed a number of PowerPoint presentations, which I have been able to draw upon in this chapter. She also authored a book called *Abuse: Questions and Answers for Counsellors and Therapists*, which is still in print, in which her answers to the questions addressed in Chapter 5 ('The effects of abuse on the practitioner') and Chapter 6 ('Service provision and supervision') are a distillation of her life's work in this particular area of practice (2003: 91–133). In acknowledging the profound influence on myself of her work, what I write here is a combination of her own ideas about supervision and my own experience; mine is less than hers in the field of abuse, but I was also an influence upon her in relation to generic supervision, in that I once supervised her work before we embarked on our relationship and marriage.

In one respect it is possible that we differed. Moira Walker always stressed the need for the supervisors of therapy and counselling in the specialist area of abuse themselves to have very good knowledge of the field of abuse if they were to be able to provide support and insight for their supervisees. I need to acknowledge that in supervising individual counsellors and supervisors as I do, as well as a group of supervisors in this special area, I do not have the wealth of experience that Moira had of working directly with abuse survivors. I was in practice a good many years before abuse came to be understood as a hidden presentation, and in those days I may have missed opportunities, other than in those comparatively rare cases where clients explicitly described such distressing experiences in their childhood or adolescence. Nevertheless, I have had considerable experience as a generic supervisor, and it is probable that I actually did learn much informally from Moira from being in such a close working relationship in our teaching together.

Yet if I have any skill at all in this area (and I think I probably have), it is because following the aspiration of all therapists and supervisors, and like those whom our profession holds in deep respect as practitioners, teachers, and writers, I have always learned most from my supervisees as well as from my clients. At times I have had to seek advice myself as to how to help supervisees handle a client who, for example, is dissociating in sessions. But I truly believe that what I have learned from most is trying to understand the client (through the supervisee), and trying to get into what is happening to the client and to the supervisee in the therapeutic relationship – sometimes getting it wrong, but sometimes getting it nearly right. I therefore suggest (although I can imagine the strains of a slight disagreement with Moira about this were she still alive) that what is necessary, above all for those who work in isolation or in agencies with survivors of abuse, is really good supervision, whether or not it initially comes from a knowledge base about abuse issues. We have to learn to be supervisors, and then we have to learn to be supervisors in the abuse field, from experience and not from head knowledge. This includes the experience of being almost completely lost, and yet hanging on to the material by the slender but strong thread of the desire to understand.

The starting point of supervision is the client, and in supervising cases of abuse, it remains the client, although the supervisee is the only person through whom we as supervisors will meet the client. The purpose of supervision is to enhance the work with the client and, if necessary, to protect the client where the counselling is either ineffective or damaging. What is also clear, and in some sense a secondary objective even if inseparable from the first, is that supervision is engaged in enhancing the counsellor's therapeutic qualities (including the core concepts of humanistic therapy), skills, knowledge, and personal abilities to undertake the work.

The reason that these two objectives, concern for the client and concern for the supervisee, are virtually inseparable is that it has long been recognized that, in working with clients, effective and non-defensive practitioners absorb, through processes variously called projection, projective identification, and transference, much that their clients carry with them, both consciously and unconsciously. It is the hidden, unconscious aspects that are the most difficult for the therapist to both recognize and process, but which a supervisor, blessed with the wisdom that comes from a certain distance from the client and the benefit of hindsight, can sometimes spot, or even experience within the supervision itself. This latter aspect of experience in the supervision session comes about because in the supervisory relationship, although less strongly and perhaps less obviously than in the counselling relationship, what has passed into the therapist from the client the therapist can now pass into the supervisor. Some have called this parallel process, although I have written elsewhere that I question the ubiquity of the term's use (Jacobs 2009: 91–103). Moira Walker used to stress the more appropriate term 'counter-transference' in all her teaching. It is a word that carries two meanings: what the client puts into and onto the counsellor, but also what the counsellor puts into and onto the client. And in supervision counter-transference involves what the supervisee puts into and onto the supervisor, as well as what the supervisor puts into and onto the supervisee.

The starting point of supervision, then, is the client – but as supervisors we soon find ourselves also reflecting upon the therapist, and upon ourselves as the supervisor. This is particularly obvious in the case of abuse, where the client has usually experienced appalling treatment from those who normally would be trusted to be selfless carers. These experiences have resulted in distortions of the nature of love, in emotional and often physical pain, and the marring of the abused person's self-image. It is all this that counsellors are drawn into, albeit at one remove, making this work far more emotionally and intellectually taxing than usual – although the same strain on the practitioner is true of those who work with severe emotional disturbance where it does not have its psychogenesis in actual abuse.

Counsellors working with this client group regularly encounter a world of agony and despair. They hear details that many in the world outside therapy would prefer to turn a deaf ear to – and indeed may well have done when the client previously approached family members or professionals in their search for help. Therapists enter a realm that has too often been – and to some extent still can be – dismissed as fantasy.

Therefore, while the primary aim of supervision is to enhance and support the work of the supervisee in the interests of the client, in supervising the counselling and therapy of abuse survivors it might be said that the supervisee has equal claim to the supervisor's attention. There is a sense in which this work always carries the possibility of feeling abusive for the practitioner, as well as it once was or still is for the client. I do not mean by this that clients who are survivors of abuse are themselves abusive, although in a few cases they may, in their frustration to be understood, act in such a way. It is mistakenly thought in some circles that those who are abused are initiated into a cycle of abuse, whereby they will in turn go on to abuse others. This is of course a fallacy: while it is often true that those who abuse may well have been abused themselves, it does not follow from that premise that all survivors of abuse become abusive. Some may, and yet it is unlikely to be those who seek therapy. Nor is it right to suggest that those who have been abused will, in rather different ways, actually mean to abuse their therapist. Even where a client rages at the counsellor, and appears to seek to reduce the therapist to emotional pulp, this is more likely to be in response to what the client has experienced in the past; they can now, at last, in the safety of the therapeutic environment, pour out their pent-up feelings, which can include rage as much as intense distress. The therapist may become a scapegoat on occasion, but in such circumstances, it is often the safety valve of therapy that enables this to occur. Likewise, supervision must become a safe place for the effects of therapy on the counsellor or therapist to be voiced, as much as the effect of abuse on the client.

The effect of the work on supervisees

My argument is that although supervisees may therefore experience in themselves, in some measure, the effects of abuse on those whom they counsel, this is not a deliberate or calculated retaliation on the part of the client, unless of course the therapist is inept. Therapy may become a place where the client's inner turmoil is acted out (although technically this is known as 'acting in'). This again is where the supervisee requires the care and support of the supervisor, if such strong emotional stirrings are not to disrupt both the work and the inner life of the supervisee. We know that the personal relationships of counsellors can be affected, including in their sexual expression; that hearing how clients have been betrayed by people they should have been able to trust most, can sow seeds of doubt about the trustworthiness of counsellors' relationships, or those of their children and partners.

If ordinary members of the public, reading about teachers, entertainers, police officers and lawyers, priests and parents being charged with sexual offences with minors, begin to wonder what goes on behind closed doors, it is not difficult to imagine how strongly the stories they hear can affect counsellors and therapists in their view of the world and the people around them. Counsellors can begin to think that nothing is what it seems, that behind the net curtains of people's lives there must be hidden other such dreadful secrets. Sometimes working with such material is more distressing than the counsellor is able to acknowledge even to themselves, let alone to their partner, friends and family – and of course the need to respect confidentiality means that they do not necessarily share their experience even in a more general way. The painful secrets of the client can become the distressing secrets of the counsellors.

Moira Walker, in her teaching over the years, would list different examples of the effects this work can have upon supervisees – signs that a supervisor needs to be on the watch for and which, together, make a formidable list for supervisors to monitor:

- Anxiety in the therapist's relationships, especially with partners and children
- Feelings of inadequacy and hopelessness about the work – which may be specific to one client or spread out to the work generally
- Feelings of helplessness and powerlessness
- Feeling attacked by the client
- Wanting to rescue the client and meet all their unmet needs
- The dulling of feeling, emotional overload or emotional exhaustion
- Tiredness
- Diminution of capacity to empathize
- The opposite – deep shock and intense emotional reactions
- Difficulty in, and fear of speaking and talking about, what is happening – the counsellor feels isolated, alienated, and 'frozen'
- Disturbing erotic or sexual feelings
- Putting in extra time or giving extra attention to a particular client, extending the usual boundaries with a deleterious effect on both counsellor and client
- Difficulty believing the client, because stretching belief actually undermines the sense of world order
- Dreading sessions either with particular clients or in general

- Losing clients prematurely
- The sense of being haunted, with no relief
- Symptoms of post-traumatic stress disorder
- Disappearing cases – cases not presented for supervision
- Cases that may not disappear but where there is a reluctance to give detail
- Talking about clients in accurate theoretical terms but not reporting their feelings – this can be difficult to spot
- Supervisee feeling supervisor is unable to cope, unwilling to understand, or is seen as vulnerable or lacking in sufficient skills
- Supervisee being over-sensitized to the wellbeing, health, and coping abilities of their supervisor.

She would also observe that these feelings could be experienced by supervisors when working with counsellors in this particular field of work. She identified other feelings that could apply to the supervisor independently:

- Sleepiness
- Difficulty in being attentive
- Restlessness and boredom
- Unconscious collusion between supervisee and supervisor.

While these effects may be a reflection of a particular client, and therefore manifest themselves in a limited way, sometimes the work with one very difficult client can have an effect that spreads out to other work; or these effects can be cumulative, rising out of the work with a number of abuse survivors. There is much to be said for any therapist's caseload being a mixed one: short and long term, varying degrees of disturbance in the client group, and a spread of presenting issues – one of the tasks of a supervisor is to keep an eye on caseloads through an overview of the supervisee's working week.

What is important to recognize here is that it is not sufficient to stop at linking the supervisee's present disturbing feelings to the client's past or present experience, but to ensure that space is given to supervisees to process what is happening to them. Supervisors may be tempted to make smart interpretations of clients, but supervising abuse means paying attention to the pain of the client and the pain of the supervisee. It is not sufficient, for example, where a supervisee is in training and therefore having personal therapy, simply to advise, or even insist, that the supervisee take their own disturbing reactions to therapy; or to suggest to a qualified supervisee, who appears to be struggling, that they should return to personal therapy. If the supervisor can provide the same containing support that would be expected of a therapist working with a client, then it is going to be more possible to engage in the process of supervising the work with the client and, initially acknowledging the impact on the supervisee, to pass then from the experience of the supervisee back to the client. The principle of therapy, to move from the here-and-now to the there-and-then, and vice versa, applies just the same to supervision.

The difficulties and anxieties inevitably aroused in counsellors and therapists who work with abuse survivors need therefore to be prepared for, both in training and in the preliminary stages of supervision. Supervision needs to provide sufficient time for reflection on the client, on the therapeutic relationship, and on the supervisee. This reflection at times may need to be extended to the supervisory relationship as well, to discuss how the supervisee is experiencing the supervision itself. Whether or not this becomes an explicit discussion, the supervisory task also involves the supervisor monitoring her or his own response to what the supervisee reports, checking whether the supervisor's feelings are a reflection of either the client or the supervisee, or both.

Working with the stresses upon the supervisee naturally brings benefits. Disillusioned counsellors are of little use to their clients. Over-involved therapists will probably create difficulties in the future for their clients. Validation of the supervisee's work will in all likelihood trickle down to greater confidence in the client. Valuing the therapist will go some way towards helping the client feel valued. Acting to limit the amount an exhausted supervisee takes on will lessen the risk of inadequate attention to present and future clients.

Fear, blame, and shame in the supervisee

This bedrock of care and support enables the other important aspects of supervision to function. Supervision is a place for unpacking the therapy itself, in an attempt to shine light both on what the client expresses in words and gestures, as well as on the practice and interventions of the counsellor, in relation to the specific material and mood brought to therapy each week by the client. The more this can be shared in supervision, the greater the opportunity for insight. Supervisees sometimes fear supervision as a place where they will be shown up as falling short. They may present their work in such a way as to forestall or mitigate any criticism that they are already feeling in themselves, and do not wish to be made explicit by their supervisor. It might be compared to the fear felt by those who are abused as children, that they are to blame for what has gone wrong. Yet supervision needs to be an open and honest forum. Abuse has nearly always involved keeping secrets, yet supervisees who keep secrets back from their supervisor prevent change from taking place. Without openness between the supervisor and supervisee, exploration of the therapeutic interaction becomes impossible. There needs to be room for disagreement, but at the same time a supervisor is likely to have pertinent, relevant, and correct interventions and suggestions to make.

What needs to be encouraged is a willingness on the part of the supervisee to consider interventions without becoming defensive. Since it is difficult not to be defensive about one's clients and one's work, supervisors need to work towards lessening defensiveness, seeking a relationship where there is no blame, just an honest attempt to understand the material.

In one of her unpublished lectures, Moira Walker put it this way:

A relationship has to be created in which the supervisee is able to speak about what is most difficult and most perplexing. They need to be able to communicate both the frightening and hidden world of the client and the sometimes frightening and worrying responses they can experience. There is otherwise a danger that the previously unspoken secrets of the client become the unspeakable experience of the counsellor. A key role of supervision is to prevent the isolation of the counsellor mirroring the isolation of the client.

What a supervisor needs to know

If this approach to supervision, and in particular to the supervision of abuse, is vital, there are nonetheless aspects of working with abuse that a supervisor will need to incorporate into their work – knowledge that it is important to acquire, and particular features that it is necessary to take into account in supervision.

First and most obviously, to return to that question of priorities in a supervisor, hard on caring for the supervisee (and an essential part of that care) are specific presentations of which the supervisor must have some knowledge, understanding, and sympathy. These might be listed as the recognition of dissociation as different from repression; of multiple personality; and of post-traumatic stress.

There are, of course, some disputes in the area of abuse over such issues as memory, no memory and false memory, and multiple personality or dissociative identity disorder (DID). Moira Walker recognized this in the valuable text she co-edited with a survivor of abuse, someone who could clearly describe her different personalities (Walker and Antony-Black 1999). Supervisors must nonetheless be open to the possibility of such presentations. They will be of little value to their supervisees if, in the words of one experienced therapist in relation to her supervisor, '[she] did not believe in dissociation', despite the supervisee presenting several cases of that kind.

The distinction between dissociation and repression is an important one: 'dissociation can be seen as a continuum where it can be a pathological mechanism (at the extreme end of this is multiple personality) through to a healthily and normally adaptive defence' (Walker 2003: 49). Similarly, DID must be part of a supervisor's vocabulary. It may be difficult to spot, but indicators of this possible pathology include an

> ... *inability to remember periods of time or life events; considerable doubt about what is real and not real; forgetting what a previous session was about; forgetting to come to sessions. In both these instances it could be because another personality was present; or self-presentation that varies in an extreme manner from session to session (clothes, hairstyle, mannerisms, tone of voice and vocabulary, likes and dislikes, level of self-confidence, content, can all be at remarkable variance).*
> (Walker 2003: 53–4)

Less contentious but equally liable to be faced by counsellors working with survivors of abuse are questions of how to respond to flashbacks, or to obvious indications of self-harm. Many of these difficult presentations are addressed, briefly but nevertheless concisely, in the third part of Moira Walker's *Abuse: Questions and Answers for*

Counsellors and Therapists (2003: 41–66). Yet she would be the first to admit that while knowledge of these matters is important for the supervisor, what is even more important is the ability to locate such knowledge in the experience of the client and the supervisee; every situation is different and there can be no standard answer to how to understand and deal with these presentations. Here, the skill of a supervisor to address questions that may help the supervisee understand the meaning of particular instances that arise in the course of therapy is valuable: 'What is it in the history of your client that might help us understand possible reasons for the need to dissociate? What has arisen in recent counselling sessions that might help explain why the client is able to present that now? What do we know about the client that could point to a way of addressing the issue?'

Certainly my experience as a supervisor in this field has been that any theoretical knowledge that I have is useful only inasmuch as it can be applied to the interaction that a supervisee is reporting; and that together we need to look at what might have been the most effective responses to date; or what responses might be tried out, at the right time and in the right tone of voice, in future sessions. Much of the time a supervisee and supervisor are as much in the dark as the client is, and it is only through tentative, intuitive responses, some of which have no effect, others of which suggest a way forward, that a therapist can be helped to enable her client to shine a little more light on their experience and on their ways of coping. Working with survivors of abuse defies any quick fix, six-session blast at their issues. Agencies and individual therapists who can offer long-term work know that the process cannot be hurried, but that it moves slowly, step by tentative step, towards some kind of resolution which is not perfect, but which provides the basis for the client, no longer in therapy, to implement and experience change.

In such theoretical matters it is clear that supervisors and supervisees need to share a common knowledge base.

It is axiomatic, at least to a psychodynamic approach, as well as many integrative therapies, that a supervisor should be well versed in theories of child development, including attachment theory. The concept of counter-transference may go under different names in various modalities, and therefore be part of supervision talk, but it is important for supervision in the field of abuse to be aware of the complexities of counter-transference, the inter-penetration, inter-subjectivity of the therapeutic and the supervisory relationship. Equally valuable is an awareness of secondary traumatization and the symptoms of post-traumatic stress disorder (PTSD). In one of her workshops, Moira Walker defined secondary traumatization as 'arising from distressing counter-transferences which become traumatizing, as opposed to being informative and helpful'. She identified such circumstances as being:

- When the counter-transference produces feelings in the therapist that are deeply discordant with their sense of self
- When they are deeply unacceptable or shocking
- Or when such feelings are unrecognized, unspoken, and defended against
- When the client's material challenges or overthrows the counsellor's view of the world and raises questions about values that are held dear
- When the material resonates too closely with unresolved personal issues, especially involving trauma
- Or when such material is encountered too frequently to allow processing to take place
- When the workload is too little supported
- When their training has not prepared counsellors sufficiently for this demanding work
- And a salutary reminder of the need for good supervision – when supervision is not good enough.

There is much to be said for pairs, threes or group supervision of those who are working with survivors of abuse. The first distinct advantage over one-to-one supervision is that the dynamic of the secret twosome, so prevalent in abuse, is diminished by sharing work with other practitioners in addition to the supervisor. Group supervision can also alleviate the isolation so commonly experienced in this work, as well as providing a valuable forum for sharing ideas, feelings, experience, and strategies. Working in isolation imposes a greater toll that being able to appreciate that others encounter similar dynamics, and might share similar counter-transference reactions, may alleviate. In some agencies where there are a variety of modalities due to counsellors coming from different training backgrounds, this mix in a group also enriches the possibilities for understanding; it increases the possibilities for more integrative strategies in working with particular presentations such as those referred to above. Clearly, pairs or group work benefits from a supervisor or facilitator who can model sharing personal reactions honestly to the clients discussed, including those that might otherwise be thought undesirable in a 'trained' and 'well-balanced' practitioner.

In a book that arises from the work of an agency, it is important to add that a supervisor supervising counsellors who work in such a setting needs to consider the dynamics of the agency itself. Some agencies will insist that supervisors work from within the agency, although there will be supervisors inevitably who work with counsellors who practise in an agency, but who themselves are not part of the organization. Just as group supervision can be extremely beneficial to counsellors working with survivors of abuse, so an agency can provide support and safety to its staff. Moira Walker described this well in a chapter entitled 'Working with abused clients in an institutional setting: holding hope amidst despair' (1996), where she highlighted the need to acknowledge the effects or impact of the structure and attitudes of the agency on the work. Organizational factors can intensify the already difficult nature of working in the context of abuse – factors such as lack of clarity and transparency in the agency's procedures and policies; or where an employing organization does not recognize the complex dynamics created by abuse; or in some ways even replicates those very dynamics. Counsellors working in agencies or institutional settings can become demoralized and feel a kind of abuse when power relationships are not sufficiently acknowledged and worked with; where there is role confusion or lack of control of caseloads, poor communication, and insufficient consultation leading to poor working relationships. There may even be in some institutions (although it might be hoped against hope not in counselling agencies themselves) a blame culture, bullying, or racial and sexual harassment.

Supervisors may therefore have a vital role to play in monitoring the conditions in which their supervisees work, and assisting their supervisees when confronting organizational abuse. While such abuse may not be at the same level as the abuse that survivors of childhood abuse have suffered, there are enough similarities to warrant taking it into account when counsellors have to shoulder their own situations as well as carry the pain of their clients. The most obvious oversight that supervisors may have is over workloads. Working with trauma is exceptionally demanding and is done best in conjunction with undertaking other work. In agencies where this is not possible, agencies that deal solely with the effects of abuse, supervisors share with managers or service directors the responsibility for ensuring that staff do not carry too many of the most distressing cases.

Elsewhere in this book proper consideration is given to counsellors who work with clients who have initiated or triggered legal proceedings and who may have to give evidence in a court of law; and to counsellors who may themselves be called to pass over their notes, or are called to give evidence in support of their client (see Chapters 6 and 7). Agencies may have policies with regard to notes; but whether or not supervisees work in agencies, supervisors need to ensure that their supervisees are properly apprised of the need to keep detailed notes of reports of abuse that their clients have shared with them, including names and dates, and that these notes should be kept securely for very much longer than usual – there could be a call for such notes as supporting evidence many years after therapy has finished. Similarly, supervisors need to consider carefully what notes they should make about the obviously factual material that could be pertinent to any present or future court case.

Given what may seem like a catalogue of requirements in this chapter in supervising counsellors working with survivors of abuse, it would not be right to leave the supervisor feeling the weight of responsibility for counsellors and clients without stressing that supervisors too need to look after themselves. When the work is taxing, when client presentations include aspects that are new or less familiar to the supervisor, there is no shame in seeking supervision of supervision, or the services of a consultant who has particular knowledge and expertise. As Moira Walker wrote in the concluding paragraph of *Abuse: Questions and Answers for Counsellors and Therapists*: 'The ripple effect of childhood abuse is extraordinarily wide and extensive.' It will surely affect the supervisor as well as the supervisee, because 'supervision has a crucial role in ensuring this is made more manageable, does not overwhelm, does not become abusive to the counsellor, and does not add further distress to the already hurt client' (Walker 2003: 133).

This Safe Place by A.D.

*Afraid, unsure
of what I face
I am not judged
In this safe place.*

*Believed, allowed
the time and space
I tell my truth
in this safe place.*

*From fear to trust
at my own pace
I find myself
in this safe place.*

*Courageous, free
through patient grace
I now can choose
my own safe place.*

References

Ainscough, C. and Toon, K. (2000) *Breaking Free: Help for Survivors of Child Sexual Abuse*, 2nd edn. London: Insight Publications.

American Psychiatric Association (APA) (2013) *Diagnostic and Statistical Manual of Mental Disorders*, 5th edn (DSM-5). Arlington, VA: APA.

Anderson-Warren, M. and Grainger, R. (2000) *Practical Approaches to Dramatherapy: The Shield of Perseus*. London: Jessica Kingsley.

Bond, T. and Mitchels, B. (2008) *Confidentiality and Record Keeping in Counselling and Psychotherapy*. Lutterworth: BACP.

Bond, T. and Sandhu, A. (2005) *Therapists in Court: Providing Evidence and Supporting Witnesses*. Lutterworth: BACP.

Bowlby, J. (1988) *A Secure Base: Clinical Applications of Attachment Theory*. London: Routledge.

Bremner, J.D., Vythilingam, M., Vermetten, E., Southwick, S.M., McGlashan, T., Nazeer, A. et al. (2003) MRI and PET study of deficits in hippocampal structure and function in women with child sexual abuse and post traumatic disorder, *American Journal of Psychiatry*, 160: 924–32.

Bromberg, P. (2014) Multiple self-states, the relational mind, and dissociation: a psychoanalytic perspective, in P.F. Dell and J.A. O'Neill (eds.) *Dissociation and the Dissociative Disorders: DSMV and Beyond* (pp. 637–52). New York: Routledge.

Buber, M. (1923/1970) *I and Thou* (trans. W. Kaufman). Edinburgh: T. & T. Clark.

Buber, M. (1996) *I and Thou*. New York: Touchstone.

Bugental, J. (1981) *The Search for Authenticity: An Existential Analytical Approach to Psychotherapy*. New York: Irvington.

Bunting, L. (2014) Invisible victims: recorded crime and children in the UK, *Child Abuse Review*, 23: 200–13.

Cawson, P., Wattam, C., Brooker, S. and Kelly, G. (2000) *Child Maltreatment in the United Kingdom: A Study of the Prevalence of Child Abuse and Neglect.* London: NSPCC.

Cloitre, M., Cohen, L. and Koenen, K. (2006) *Treating Survivors of Childhood Abuse: Psychotherapy for the Interrupted Life.* New York: Guilford Press.

Coates, D. (2010) Impact of childhood abuse: biopsychosocial pathways through which adult mental health is compromised, *Australian Social Work*, 63: 391–403.

Cooper, M. (2005) Therapists' experiences of relational depth: a qualitative interview study, *Counselling and Psychotherapy Research*, 5 (2): 87–95.

Cooper, M. (2008) *Essential Research Findings in Counselling and Psychotherapy: The Facts are Friendly.* London: Sage.

Crown Prosecution Service (CPS) (2014) *Provision of Therapy for Vulnerable or Intimated Adult Witnesses Prior to a Criminal Trial – Practice Guidance* [available at: www.cps.gov.uk/publications/prosecution/pretrialadult.html].

Csikszentmihalyi, M. (2009) *Flow.* London: Rider.

Dell, P.F. and O'Neill, J.A. (eds.) (2014) *Dissociation and the Dissociative Disorders: DSMV and Beyond.* New York, Routledge.

Department of Health (2006) *Victims of Violence and Abuse Prevention Programme*, Delphi Report. London: Department of Health and National Institute for Mental Health in England.

Fisher, G. (2005) Existential psychotherapy with adult survivors of sexual abuse, *Journal of Humanistic Psychology*, 45: 10–40.

Fisher, J. (2014) Putting the pieces together: 25 years of learning trauma treatment, *Psychotherapy Networker*, May/June [available at: http://www.janinafisher.com/pdfs/twenty-five-years.pdf].

Fitzpatrick, M., Carr, A., Dooley, B., Flanagan-Howard, R., Flanagan, E., Tierney, K. et al. (2010) Profiles of adult survivors of severe sexual, physical and emotional institutional abuse in Ireland, *Child Abuse Review*, 19: 387–404.

Geller, S. and Greenberg, L. (2002) Therapeutic presence: therapists' experience of presence in the psychotherapy encounter, *Person-Centred and Experiential Psychotherapies*, 1 (1/2): 71–86.

Gerhardt, S. (2004) *Why Love Matters: How Affection Shapes a Baby's Brain.* Hove: Brunner-Routledge.

Gilbert, R., Spatz Widom, C., Browne, K., Fergusson, D., Webb, E. and Janson, S. (2008) Burden and consequences of child maltreatment in high-income countries, *The Lancet*, 373 (9657): 68–81.

Gilligan, S. (1997) *The Courage to Love: Principles and Practices of Self-Relations Psychotherapy.* New York: Norton.

Herman, J. (1981) *Father–Daughter Incest.* Cambridge, MA: Harvard University Press.

Herman, J. (1997) *Trauma and Recovery.* New York: Basic Books.

Irigaray, L. (1985) *This Sex Which is Not One.* New York: Cornell University Press.

Jacobs, M. (2009) *Our Desire of Unrest.* London: Karnac Books.

Kalsched, D. (1996) *The Inner World of Trauma.* London: Routledge.

Kierkegaard, S. (1844/1980) *The Concept of Anxiety* (trans. R. Thomte). Princeton, NJ: Princeton University Press.

Krug, O.T. (2009) James Bugental and Irvin Yalom: two masters of existential therapy cultivate presence in the therapeutic encounter, *Journal of Humanistic Psychology,* 49 (3): 329–54.

London, E. (1999) *Wow! Moments* [unpublished manuscript].

Mearns, D. and Cooper, M. (2005) *Working at Relational Depth in Counselling and Psychotherapy.* London: Sage.

Meekums, B. (2000) *Creative Group Therapy for Women Survivors of Child Sexual Abuse: Speaking the Unspeakable.* London: Jessica Kingsley.

MIND (2013) *Understanding Dissociative Disorders.* London: MIND.

Ministry of Justice (2015) *The Code of Practice for Victims of Crime* [available at: https://www.gov.uk/government/publications/the-code-of-practice-for-victims-of-crime].

Olio, K.A. and Cornell, W.F. (1993) The therapeutic relationship as the foundation for treatment with adult survivors of sexual abuse, *Psychotherapy: Theory, Research, Practice, Training,* 30 (3): 512–23.

Radford, L., Corral, S., Bradley, C., Fisher, H., Bassett, C., Howat, N. et al. (2011) *Child Abuse and Neglect in the UK Today.* London: NSPCC [accessed at: https://www.nspcc.org.uk/globalassets/documents/research-reports/child-abuse-neglect-uk-today-research-report.pdf].

Richardson, S. (2002) Will you sit by her side? An attachment-based approach to work with dissociative conditions, in V. Sinason (ed.) *Attachment, Trauma and Multiplicity: Working with Dissociative Identity Disorder* (pp. 150–65). Hove: Routledge.

RSPH Working Group on Arts, Health and Wellbeing (2013) *Arts, Health and Wellbeing Beyond the Millennium: How far have we come and where do we want to go?* [accessed at: https://www.rsph.org.uk/resourceLibrary/arts-health-and-wellbeing-beyond-the-millennium-how-far-have-we-come-and-where-do-we-want-to-go-.html].

Sanderson, C. (2006) *Counselling Adult Survivors of Childhood Sexual Abuse*. London: Jessica Kingsley.

Sinason, V. (2002) *Attachment, Trauma and Multiplicity: Working with Dissociative Identity Disorder*. Hove: Brunner-Routledge.

Sinason, V. (ed.) (2012a) *Trauma, Dissociation and Multiplicity: Working on Identity and Selves*. Hove: Routledge.

Sinason, V. (2012b) Introduction, in V. Sinason (ed.) *Trauma, Dissociation and Multiplicity: Working on Identity and Selves* (pp. 2–6). Hove: Routledge.

Smail, M. (2013) *Making Space for Soul Talk: Recent Research. Dramatherapy with Myth and Fairytale: The Golden Stories of Sesame*. London: Jessica Kingsley.

Spataro, J., Mullen, P., Burgess, P., Wells, D. and Moss, S. (2004) Impact of child sexual abuse on mental health: prospective study in males and females, *British Journal of Psychiatry*, 184 (4): 16–21.

Starmer, K. (2013) The criminal justice response to child sexual abuse: time for a national consensus, speech, 6 March [available at: http://www.cps.gov.uk/news/articles/the_criminal_justice_response_to_child_sexual_abuse_-_time_for_a_national_consensus].

Steele, B. (1990) Some sequelae of the sexual maltreatment of children, in H.B. Levine (ed.) *Adult Analysis and Childhood Sexual Abuse*. Hillsdale, NJ: Analytic Press.

University of York, Department of Social Policy and Social Work (1999) *Research on Adult Survivors of Childhood Sexual Abuse: A Report of the Experiences of Services*. York: North Yorkshire Health Authority.

van der Kolk, B. (2014) *The Body Keeps the Score*. London: Penguin Books.

van der Kolk, B. and McFarlane, A. (1996) The black hole of trauma, in B.A. van der Kolk, A.C. MacFarlane and L. Weisaeth (eds.) *Traumatic Stress* (pp. 3–23). New York: Guilford Press.

Walker, M. (1992) *Surviving Secrets*. Buckingham: Open University Press.

Walker, M. (1996) Working with abused clients in an institutional setting: holding hope amidst despair, in E. Smith (ed.) *Integrity and Change: Mental Health in the Marketplace*. London: Routledge.

Walker, M. (2003) *Abuse: Questions and Answers for Counsellors and Therapists*. London: Whurr.

Walker, M. and Antony-Black, J. (1999) *Hidden Selves: An Exploration of Multiple Personality*. Buckingham: Open University Press.

Winnicott, D.W. (1971) *Playing and Reality*. London: Penguin Books.

Yalom, I. (1980) *Existential Psychotherapy*. New York: Basic Books.

Index

Abuse iii
    child, cases 116
    child, scale 20
    consequences 21, 127
    cycle of 23, 146
    effects on client iii, 23, 147
    effects on counsellor 147
    emotional/psychological 44, 46
    impact of i, ii, 20, 22, 39–56, 61, 126, 127
    neglect 102
    organizational 157
    physical 46, 102
    ripple effect 158
    sexual 44–45, 46, 49, 102, 109
    society's responsibility iii
    of therapist 146
    work – effect on counsellor's 142
abusers 41, 53 (see also perpetrators)
    the abused 146
    others' complicity 109
    power 127
    survivor's reaction to conviction 125
acceptance
    of being 95
    of group members 89
    of self 54, 105–6
    of therapeutic support during trial 129
acting in 147
adaptive behaviours 58
addictions 26
    alcohol 8, 16, 23, 36, 48, 49, 55
    drugs/substance abuse 8, 16, 23, 36, 48, 49, 55

administration 34
administrator 37
advertising 28, 32
agency
    communication 157
    counselling 156–8
    effects on counsellors 157
    insufficient consultation 157
    responsibilities 157
    structure and attitudes 157
agoraphobia 23
aims of DAA 26
Ainscough, C. And Toon, K. 22
alter egos 14, 66–7
Anderson-Warren, M. And Grainger, R.G. 99
anger
    at acquittal 124
    clients' 50, 55, 70, 77, 80, 110
    at defence barrister 121
    group members' 83, 91
anti-depressants 6, 15
anti-discriminatory practice 6
anti-oppressive practice 6
anti-psychotics 6
anxiety 23
    clients' 16, 50
    therapists' 148, 150
    witnesses' 115, 122
archive 130
art 85, 89
artefacts 96
art forms 89
arts, therapeutic expressive 84, 91, 105
artwork 96
assessments 30. 34, 37

Index

attachment 12, 81
   theory 155
attendance 70, 78, 88, 103
availability of service 28
awareness raising
   of abuse 36, 37
   of self and others 83, 95

BACP – see British Association for Counselling and Psychotherapy
barrister
   defence 120, 121, 124, 132, 137
   prosecution 118, 121, 125, 137
barriers – to therapeutic relationship 67 – 71
behaviour, destructive 12, 93
Being with Others 15
bi-polar mood disorder 5
blame
   clients' experience 4, 53, 83
   culture 151, 157
   supervisees' 151
Bond, T. And Mitchels, B. 132, 136
Bond, T. And Sandhu, A. 131, 132
boundaries
   of counselling 6, 32, 57, 76
   during court case 136
   extending 148
   within group 31, 87, 102
Bournemouth Court 118
Bournemouth Police Station 111
Bournemouth University 17, 20, 25, 27
Bowlby, J. 59
brain 22
Bremner, J. D. 22
British Association for Counselling and Psychotherapy (BACP) 10, 20, 29
British Crime Survey 20
brochure 26
Buber, M. 59, 68
Bugental, J. 59
bullying 15, 50, 51, 103, 157
Bunting, L. 20, 21

carers 145
caseload 149, 157
Cawson, P. 21
CBT (see Cognitive Behavioural Therapy)
celebrities, as abusers 56
change, for client 85, 154
Charitable Incorporated Organization 34
charitable status 30, 31, 34
Charity Commission 32
Child Abuse Investigation Team 112
childcare facilities 36
child development 64, 155
childhood records 113
child parts/selves 100
child protection 20, 21
Child Protection Register 20
children iii, 20, 23, 50, 55, 56, 70, 119
child within/inner 7
choice
   disallowed/punished 91
   of disclosure 141
   reporting to police 107
   within group 87, 92, 93
church 43, 44
circle, healing 89
Cis'ters 25
Citizens' Advice 117
clarity of policies 6
clients (see also survivors)
   ambivalence 70
   attendance 70, 78, 88, 103
   background 7
   commitment 8, 9, 88
   co-morbid conditions 55
   confidence 85, 137
   consent 134–5
   counsellor's perceptions 58
   data 16
   destructive behaviours 12, 93
   differences of survivors 62, 63, 102
   dissociation 13
   distancing 87
   experiences 14, 39–56

fears 15
fitness 15
further distress 158
history 154
hostility 70
hypervigilance 58, 59
matching to counsellors 34
motivation 15
needs 12
preparation for court 133
protection 144
re-abuse 28
recovery 52–5, 85, 125
reviews 16
supervisor's role 144
support pre-trial 136
complicity 109
confidentiality 6, 29, 31, 32, 40, 61, 131, 133, 136, 148
connectedness
  between group members 15
  with clients 57, 67, 68, 69, 70, 73–5, 77, 78
  within creative groups 80, 86, 87, 89, 102
constitution of DAA 30
continuing professional development (CPD) 11
control of life 104, 105
Cooper, M. 59, 75
Co-ordinator 34
coping mechanisms/strategy 48–50, 58, 64, 65, 71, 77, 154
core group 26–7, 30–2
costs 32
counselling principles 6, 150
counsellors 10–2
  applications 10
  challenges 58, 60, 69, 70, 77
  commitment 10, 28, 30, 35
  criticism 78
  demoralization 157
  difficulties 70, 148
  dreading sessions 148
  early ending 10
  effects of work 148
  emotional overload or exhaustion 148

erotic or sexual feelings 148
experience 57–58
expertise 132
extending boundaries 148
fear, blame, shame 151
feelings 148, 155
handbook 11
induction 10
inept 147
interventions 151
introductory sessions 9
isolation 148, 152, 156
losing clients 149
modalities 156
objectivity 139
perspectives 132
qualifications 10, 28, 30
recruitment 16
registration 10
relationships 147, 148
responses to clients 154
responsibility 133
role 61
role confusion 157
skills and knowledge 10
statements to police 129, 136
symptoms of PTSD 149
validation 151
valuing 151
as witnesses 129
work enhanced 56
counsellors' notes
  court order 135
  disclosure 135, 141, 158
  process notes 132
  provided for investigation 111, 113, 129–35, 137
counter–transference 142, 145, 155, 156
court
  Crown 114
  entering 139
  order 135
  preparation for 137–8
  procedures 107
  process 129, 131, 133–4
  visit 117, 137–8

Index

CPD (see continuing professional development)
CPS (see Crown Prosecution Service)
CRB (see Criminal Records Bureau)
creative therapy groups 14, 44, 48, 51, 79–106
   benefits 86
   challenges 79, 102–4
   closure 89
   conflict 87
   criticism 87, 103
   feedback 104–5
   inclusiveness 87
   programme 85
   safe environment
   selecting participants 85–6
   structures 88–96
credibility of victims 108
crime 23, 45, 125, 132, 140, 141
criminality 22
criminal justice 128
criminal justice system 107
Criminal Records Bureau (CRB) checks 29
Crown Prosecution Service (CPS) 136
   decision to/not to prosecute 114
   lack of advice or preparation 118
   need for change 108
   proceeding to re-trial 124
   prosecution witnesses 5, 133–7
   role of 113–4
   submission of notes 129–30
   victim's entitlements 112
Csikszentmihalyi, M. 75
Cults 14
cycle of abuse 23, 146

DAA (see Dorset Action on Abuse)
dance 85, 89, 96
Daniel Ann x, 19, 27, 30
Data Protection 130

DBS (see Disclosure and Barring Service)
debrief 11, 35
defence 118, 120, 139
defences, protective 54, 57, 64–7
Dell, P.F. and O'Neill, J.A. 13
denial 23, 58,
   of guilt 119, 120
depression 16, 22, 23, 42, 52
despair 94, 146
destructive behaviour 93, 103
detachment 68–9, 73, 74, 77
diagnosis 13, 14, 86
Diagnostic and Statistical Manual of Mental Disorders 66
diagnostic labels 86
dialectical behaviour therapy 6
diazepam 6
DID (see dissociative identity disorder)
Directions Hearing 136
Director of Public Prosecutions 108
directory of services 26
disadvantage of survivors 20
Disclosure
   by clients 3, 4–5, 36
   of evidence 114, 131, 141
   by group members 95, 102
Disclosure and Barring Service 10
dissociation 9, 40, 46, 50, 58, 66, 70, 77, 86, 95, 152, 154
dissociative conditions/disorders/phenomena/processes 5, 13–4, 17, 18, 23, 80, 86, 101, 103, 153
dissociative identity disorder (DID) 23, 101, 153
distress 92, 94, 103, 146
disturbance, emotional 146
dog, therapy 89
domestic violence 21
Dorset 13, 20, 24, 25, 27, 112, 123
Dorset Action on Abuse xiii, 4, 19–20, 25–34 (see also Hurting to Healing)
drama 85, 89, 103

dreams 93
drugs 36, 48, 49, 55, 108

eating disorders 8, 16, 22
education failure 23
electric shock therapy 52
emotional distress 9
emotions, evoked 87
emotions, processing 22
ending 71
ending review 10, 16
environment
    safe 86, 146
    non-judgemental 87
equal opportunities 34
ethical principles 6
ethnic origin 25
evaluation 15–7, 53
evidence 114, 115, 117, 133, 137
    counsellors' notes 158
    discrediting 132
    documentary 111
    forensic 108
    giving 120–3
    potential 131
    relevant 136
    reliability 134
    supporting 108
    tainted 134, 138, 140
expert witness 116, 131
expression within creative group 89, 95
    abstract 102
    authentic 90
    metaphorical 90, 102
    of personal experience 102
    symbolic 90, 93, 102

facilitators of groups 14, 31, 35, 86, 90, 102, 103, 105
factual material 158
family
    defendant's 122, 123
    relationships 16, 17, 61, 105
    survivors' 50, 55, 64, 146
father 47, 49, 52, 87
fear 4, 160
    after court case 124, 127
    clients' 4, 15, 44, 48, 53, 80, 87
    creative group members' 83, 93, 103
    supervisee's 151–2
feedback 29, 38, 104
film 85, 89
financial accountability 34
financial security 25
Finch, Gillian 25
First Person Plural 117
Fisher, G. 60
Fisher, J. 84
fitness, physical 15
Fitzpatrick, M. 22
flashbacks 3, 8, 9, 16, 43, 50, 54, 103, 115, 153
flow 75
formative years 60
fragility of clients 57, 58, 62
frames of understanding 84
freedom 54, 98
free sessions 28
friends 16, 17, 23
Friends of Hurting to Healing 37
From Hurting to Healing 29, 31
Full Code Test 114, 128
funders 15
funding 24, 31, 34, 36, 37
fundraising 18, 33, 37

Geller, S. and Greenberg, L. 75
gender 25
general practitioners 5, 10, 44, 51
Gerhardt, S. 60
Gilbert, R. 21
Gilligan, S. 80
GP (see general practitioners)
grief 54
grooming 109, 122
grounding closure 89
ground rules 31, 87, 91
group(s)
    academic interest 26
    agreement 102
    creative therapy 79–106
    core 27, 31, 35
    discussion 29
    facilitated 14

fledgling 25
parenting 36
self-help support 31, 34
supervisors' 35
therapeutic 16, 79
group supervision 142, 156
Guidelines on Presenting Cases of Child Sexual Abuse 128
guilt 44, 113, 116

handbook 11
harassment, racial and sexual 157
harm, protection from 59
healing 78, 100
healing circle 89
healing process 59, 60
health professionals 27
help, search for 146
Herman, J. 13, 60
historical cases 112, 113
HM Courts and Tribunal Service (HMCTS) 112
holistic approach 86
homelessness 22, 23, 26
hope 74, 84–5, 141
hopes 8, 93
hostility of clients 70
Howe, Kate x, 19–38
Hubbard-Ford, Rosa x, 39–56
Hurting to Healing xiii, 2–18, 34–38, 39, 43, 45, 52–4, 78, 109, 115, 130, 133, 134 (see also Dorset Action on Abuse)
hypervigilance 58,59

IAPT (see Increasing Access to Psychological Therapies)
ice breaker 89
I –it relating 68
imagination, developing 85
imagining 93
impact of abuse 21–3, 126, 127
impeachment 132
improvements after counselling 16
improvisation 97–8
incest 25

inclusiveness 87
Increasing Access to Psychological Therapies (IAPT) 5, 24
induction of counsellors 6
inhibitions 98
initial meeting with clients 6
insomnia 23
insurance, personal indemnity 10
integrative strategies 156
integrative therapies 155
intellectual development 23
inter-penetration 155
interpersonal skills 60, 67
inter-subjectivity 155
interventions
    counsellor's 151
    supervisor's 151
interviews
    with counsellors 58
    with police 111, 112, 117, 129, 134
    DVD recordings of 117, 118
In the Beginning 82
intimidation 119
introductory period 8, 9–10
invalidation 46–7, 124
investigation 112–3, 114, 115, 127
invitation 93, 96–101, 104
Irigary, L. 82
isolation
    clients' 16, 40, 48
    counsellors' 152, 156
I-Thou relating 68, 72

Jacobs, M. 145
Jacobs, Professor Michael v, x–xi, 142–58
John Lewis Partners 33
journal for creative group members 89
journey of creative group 95
judge 116, 120, 121–2, 125, 126, 136, 140
judgement
    non-judgemental 87
    of survivors 15, 48, 61, 127
    within groups 102

judicial process 107–28, 129–41, 130, 131
jury 124, 139
justice 141

Kalsched, D. 60, 70
Kierkegaard, S, 73
knowledge, supervisor's need for 143
Krug, O.T. 59

Lancet, The 21
leap of faith 72, 73, 78
learning, difficulties in 22
legal process
    conference topic 36
    contamination 131
    notes for 142
liaison volunteer 18
liberation
    from rigidity 83
    through soundscaping 98
lifeline of connections 74
liminal realm, in creative group 89
listening, in creative group 93
London, E. 73
loneliness 16, 65
Longhurst, Gail xi, 129–41
long-term therapy 5–6, 14, 28, 43, 74, 154
    access to 24
    caseloads 149
    free 23
    need for 23, 24, 54, 63–4, 86, 127
Lottery funding 8, 33, 34, 37
love, distortion of 145

Maguire, Ellie x, 107–28
mask making 52, 98–101
masks 98, 99, 103
    survivors' 49, 50, 64, 66, 91, 99, 101
    uses of 100–1
McFarlane, E. 61
Mearns, D. and Cooper, M. 59, 67, 68
medical records 111, 113

medication 6, 15, 44, 55, 84
Meekums, B. 86, 92
memories 5, 84, 87, 94, 132
memory 22, 153
    false 153
mental health 15, 20, 22, 23, 24
    diagnosis 86
metaphors 90, 95
MIND 13
Ministry of Justice 112
modalities of counselling 156
models of counselling 12
monitoring outcomes 16–7
mother 46, 47, 49, 50, 51, 52, 60, 81, 94
motivation of clients 15, 112
mood swings 8, 16
movement, in creative groups 85, 89, 103
multiple personality 13, 152, 153
music with creative groups 85, 89, 97, 103
My Safe Place 88

National Health Service 5, 6, 7, 9, 17, 24, 28, 36, 54
National Society for the Prevention of Cruelty to Children 21, 111
networking 25
NHS (see National Health Service)
nightmares 8, 50, 54, 94
NSPCC (see National Society for the Prevention of Cruelty to Children

objectivity of counsellor 139
obstacles faced by counsellor 58, 70, 77
Officer in Charge (OIC) 112
Olio, K.A. and Cornell, W.F. 60
outreach 17–8

paedophile ring 14
pain
    of client 150
    clinics 5

Index

emotional 145
physical 145
of supervisor 150
panic attacks 16, 22, 50
parachute 92
parallel process 145
parenting difficulties 22, 36
participants in creative groups 79–105,
   feedback 104–5
partner relationships 16, 17, 23, 55, 101
past
   focus in therapy 6
   influence of 84
payment 8, 37
perfectionism 49, 55
perpetrators 108, 120, 127, (see also abusers)
   counselling for 11
   disclosure of 111
   of notoriety 119
   pre-sentence report 126
personality disorders 5, 14
phobias 8, 16
physical activity 15
physical health 8
Pittman, Matthew 56
play 96–7, 99, 100, 101
poems 83, 84–5, 90, 94–5, 97
poetry 85, 89, 94
polarization with groups 102, 103
police 5, 115, 135
   access to information 134, 135
   investigation 112–3
   poor protection 127
   reporting to 107, 108, 111, 129–30, 134
   thanks 125

policies 6, 34, 157
Pool, Dr. Zoë xi, 2–18, 79–106, 104, 107–28
Poole Community Mental Health Team (CMHT) 28, 29, 30
Poole Mental Health Social Services 27–8

post-traumatic stress disorder (PTSD)
   clients' diagnosis 5
   consequences of abuse 22, 23
   of counsellors 149
   manifested by clients 54
   signs of 7
   supervisors' recognition of 152, 155
power relationships 157
practice guidance 135, 136
premises, DAA 31, 33
pre-sentence report 126
press 115, 119, 123, 127
pre-therapy stage 71, 72, 77
primary care 26
principles 6, 28, 79
private counselling practice 24, 54, 134
Probation Service 5
procedures,
   agency 157
   court 107
process, individual and group 96
professionals, caring 56, 146
professional standards 37
projection 145
projective identification 145
prosecution 114
prostitution 22
protection of self 59, 70
protective defences 57, 64, 67
psyche 80
psychic split 70
psychiatrist 5, 10, 13, 24, 42, 44, 116
psychodynamic approach 155
psychogenesis 146
psychosexual therapists 5
psychotic disorders 23
psychotropic drugs 44
public awareness 18
public gallery 117
punishing choice 91
puppets 103
Putman, F.W. 60

qualifications of counsellors 10
quality of life of clients 16, 54

racial harassment 157
Radford, L. 20
rage 75, 103, 146
rape 126, 140
Rape Crisis 5
re-abuse 28, 36
reality, for group members 83
record-keeping 34
recovery 52–5, 85, 125
recruitment 10, 16
references 10
referral 5–6, 25
reflections, in creative groups 83, 87, 89, 93
refuges 36
rejection of survivors 15, 100
relating, patterns of 70, 87
relational beings 58–60
relational depth 67, 68, 76, 77
relationships 59, 84
    clients' 40, 50, 53, 61, 62, 63, 66, 68
    co-dependent 105
    power 157
    supervisory 155
    support group's 31
    survivors' 23, 59
    working 157
relationship, therapeutic (see therapeutic relationship)
reliability 108
religion 49
remembering, in creative group 93
reporting abuse 3, 107, 109–12
repression 152
reprisals 127
rescuing client 148
research 21, 22, 27, 64
resilience of survivors 53, 78
resources 26, 54, 127–8
respect
    for clients 6, 77
    in group 87
    from police 111
responsibility, society's iii
restructuring DAA 30
results of counselling 17
Rethink 36

review 15–7
Richardson, Sue 12
Richmond Fellowship 36
rigidity
    liberation from 83
    of beliefs 103
risk
    within creative therapy 83, 87, 105
    for victims of abuse 108
ritual abuse 14, 100
Rochdale 108
Royal Society for Public Health (RSPH) 15

safe environment 79, 86–96, 100
safeguarding 34
safe place/space 88, 80, 147, 160
safe practice 6, 34
safety 3, 87, 110
    in facilitated groups 14
    primary concern 14, 102, 103
    survivors' sense of 58, 60
    in therapeutic relationship 12, 76
Samaritans 5, 27
Sanderson, Christiane 22
SARC (see Sexual Assault Referral Centre)
Savile, Jimmy 108, 109, 110
schizophrenia 5
school 50
screen in court 115
Seaforth House 3–4
secrets 53, 54, 81, 109, 147, 148, 151
security 55, 58, 119
self 39, 42, 80, 81
self-awareness 80, 81, 95
self-consciousness 71, 97
self-discovery 85
self-esteem 15, 16, 17, 53
self-expression 15, 82, 83, 86
self-harm 3, 7, 16, 22, 23, 36, 49, 55, 153
self-help groups 14, 31
self-image 145
self-isolation 104

self-protective behaviour 59, 67, 70
self-referrals 5
self-reflection 64
sensitivity of counsellors 63
sentencing 125, 126
Service Director xi, 37, 157
sex as self-harm 55
Sexual Assault Referral Centre (SARC) 112
sexual difficulties 22, 42, 49, 50
sexual harassment 157
sexual offences 147
Sexual Offences Act 1956 111
shame 4, 15, 48, 84, 87, 124
  counsellors' 151
silence(s) 9, 97–8
silenced 92, 94
Sinason, V. 13, 60, 63
singing 97–8
sketch book 89
sleeping difficulties 16
Smail, M. 80, 89
social class 25
social events 18
social
  exclusion 20, 23
  functioning 23
  interaction 15
  isolation 14
  withdrawal 16
Social Services 5, 36
social workers 27
society iii, 55, 56
soma 80
soundscaping 97–8
Southampton
space
  safe 89
  therapeutic 76, 80
  transitional 96
Spataro, J. 22
specialized field of counselling 27, 43, 62–4
special measures in court 115, 116, 117
Starmer, Keir 108, 128
statistics 15, 16, 21, 22, 125

stigma 14
storytelling 85, 89, 103
stress
  of supervisee 150
  of witness 116, 118
structures in creative group 88–91
struggle of survivors 83
student counsellors 11
substance
  abuse/misuse 8, 16, 22
  addiction 23
suicidal ideation 5, 36, 42, 50, 55
suicide 5, 22
supervisees
  care of 142
  fear, blame and shame 151–2
  feelings 150
  knowledge 154
  pain 150
  personal therapy 150
  validation 151
supervision 142–58
  counsellor's need 69, 133
  current practice 35
  DAA policies 34
  early practice 26, 29, 30
  group 11, 12, 142, 156
  for group facilitators 14
  mixed modalities 12, 156
  for supervisors 142, 158
supervisors 11, 12, 142–58
  crucial role 157, 158
  consider dynamics of agency 156
  interventions 151
  knowledge 152, 154, 155
  need for self-care 158
  notes 158
  personal reactions 156
  priorities 152
  skills 154
  supervisees' opinion 149
  support for court witnesses 133, 134, 141
  support for supervisee 146, 150
survival through dissociation 80
Surviving Secrets 27

survivors 2–18, 39–56, (see also clients)
  adaptive, self-protective behaviour 70
  courage 78
  dedication to iii
  developing services 25, 26, 27
  disadvantaged 20
  effects of abuse 20, 23
  experience of judicial process 107–27
  limits of talking therapies 81
  need for long-term help 24
  perceived as abusive to counsellor 146
  presentations at conferences 36
  target audience for conference 36
  tenacity 78

talking therapy limitations 80, 81, 84
template, Hurting to Healing for others 53
tension, released through creative work 95
test, for survivor in group 104
testing the relationship 71, 72, 73, 77
therapeutic relationship 12, 58, 60–2
  barriers 67–71
  connection 73–6
  development 71–3
  pre-therapy stage 77–8
  stages 57
  time to establish 63
therapy, creative 79–106
third party material 113, 114
This Safe Place 160
threats, anticipated by survivors 82
time 57, 62, 63
  importance of 57
  limited sessions 80
  longer needed 62, 63, 67
tiredness of counsellor 148
Toon, K. 22

training 10, 18, 26, 30, 33, 35–6, 54, 55
  for social work students 17
transference 145
transitional space 96
transition, in creative groups 89, 95, 100
trauma 23, 61, 68, 83, 84
  victims 80
  working with 157
traumatisation, secondary 142, 155
trial 114–7, 120–3, 125–6
triggers 46, 81
  of distress or flashbacks 95, 103
  to identify childhood abuse 36
trust
  admiration for clients' 62, 77
  being with self and others 85
  building 57, 59, 61, 72, 87
  difficulties 9, 15, 45, 58, 60, 62, 63
  in police 113
  in safe place 160
  taking time 72
  within therapeutic relationship 12, 78
trustees 32

unemployment 23, 53
university academics 27
University of York 23, 24

validation
  in creative therapy 95, 101
  of supervisee 151
van der Kolk, B. 60–61
verdict 124–7
  majority 124
  not guilty 116
  waiting for 129, 139–40
vicious circle 67–8
victim impact statement 126
victim mode 55, 65
Victim Personal Statement (VPS) 126

victims
    after trial 127
    of childhood abuse 108
    in court 118, 120, 122, 123
    of crime 112, 114
    evidence in chief 117
    Savile's 110
    support during trial 115
Victims Code 118
Victims' Right to Review
    Scheme 114
Victim Support 5, 138
violation 81, 83, 91, 113
violence 20-1, 83
visualization, creative 93, 103
VIW (see vulnerable or
    intimidated witnesses)
voice, in creative group 85, 89
voluntary organisations 24, 36
volunteers 10-2, 30, 117
vulnerability
    of a child 109
    of clients 62, 63, 70
vulnerable or intimidated
    witnesses (VIW) 116, 118,
    128, 134

Walker, Dr. Moira iii, 3, 7, 11, 12,
    22, 142, 145, 148, 152, 153,
    155, 156, 158
    beginnings of DAA 19, 20, 25,
    27, 28, 30
Walker, M. and Antony-Black, J. 153

warm-up, in creative group
    89, 92
weight 15
welcome, in creative group 89
well-being, in creative group 85
whistle-blower 110
Winnicott, D. W. 96
Witness Care Units 112
Witness Charter 117, 128
witnesses 117, 118, 119, 120,121,
    138
    vulnerable or intimidated 116,
    118, 128, 134
witnessing, in creative group 93
witness of fact 131, 132, 133
Witness Service 117-8
witness stand 129, 138-9
Witness Support 118, 125
women survivors 30
work
    clients' 16, 17, 53, 119
    effect on counsellors 147-51
    inability to maintain 22
    with client 61, 144
workaholism 49, 55
workloads 157
wounds, survivors' 83

Yalom, I. 59
Youth Justice and Criminal
    Evidence Act 116

Zoega, Jane xi, 57-78